# DATE DUE

| | | | |
|---|---|---|---|
| | | | |
| | | | |
| | | | |
| | | | |
| | | | |
| | | | |
| | | | |
| | | | |
| | | | |
| | | | |
| | | | |
| | | | |
| | | | |
| | | | |
| | | | |
| | | | |
| | | | |
| | | | |

Demco, Inc. 38-293

JUL 27 2012

# THE FINCH EFFECT

# THE FINCH EFFECT

## THE FIVE STRATEGIES TO ADAPT AND THRIVE IN YOUR WORKING LIFE

Nacie Carson

**JOSSEY-BASS**
A Wiley Imprint
www.josseybass.com

Published by Jossey-Bass
A Wiley Imprint
One Montgomery Street, Suite 1200, San Francisco, CA 94104-4594
www.josseybass.com

Jossey-Bass books and products are available through most bookstores. To contact Jossey-Bass directly call our Customer Care Department within the U.S. at 800-956-7739, outside the U.S. at 317-572-3986, or fax 317-572-4002.

Wiley publishes in a variety of print and electronic formats and by print-on-demand. Some material included with standard print versions of this book may not be included in e-books or in print-on-demand. If this book refers to media such as a CD or DVD that is not included in the version you purchased, you may download this material at http://booksupport.wiley.com. For more information about Wiley products, visit www.wiley.com.

Library of Congress Cataloging-in-Publication Data

Carson, Nacie, 1985—
   The finch effect : the five strategies to adapt and thrive in your working life / Nacie Carson. – 1
   p. cm.
Includes index.
   ISBN 978-1-118-13428-3 (hardback)
   ISBN 978-1-118-22521-9 (ebk.)
   ISBN 978-1-118-23865-3 (ebk.)
   ISBN 978-1-118-26330-3 (ebk.)
   1.   Success in business.  2.   Career development.  3.   Self-actualization (Psychology)   I. Title.
   HF5386.C332 2012
   650.1—dc23                                                                    2012003658

Printed in the United States of America
FIRST EDITION

HB Printing            10  9  8  7  6  5  4  3  2  1

# contents

*This book is dedicated to the great teachers of my life:*
*my father, David, who taught me how to succeed;*
*my mother, Shelley, who taught me how to dream;*
*my brother, Dave, who taught me how to laugh;*
*and my dear Charles, who taught me how to love.*

# foreword

I was surprised when Nacie Carson asked me to write the foreword for this book. After all, I'm a nerd; I don't consider myself an entrepreneur. Then she explained that she thought craigslist was a big part of something she called the "gig economy," and it was helping people deal with the changes that have taken place in jobs and employment over the past several years. She even said she'd used the site herself as a source for clients when she was a freelancer.

That sounded familiar. After many years with IBM and then some with Charles Schwab, I was a computer systems freelancer myself when I started craigslist back in 1995. But I didn't start craigslist to find a job or clients. I started it as an email list to let people know about arts and technology events happening in San Francisco.

Things grew from there. I started getting emails from people for all kinds of things—apartments, jobs, stuff they wanted to sell or trade. I wrote code which turned the emails into web pages to make them easier to review. More and more of them came in, and I handled all of them from my San Francisco flat, although I had some volunteers helping me in 1998.

A lot of people who were new to the Internet came to our site and got something done. That showed people the Internet was actually useful and easy to use. Eventually people started telling me to monetize the site and charge for all the listings like other sites were doing. They didn't understand. A lot of people need a break. Giving most of them a free way to get something they need can make all the difference to them.

As I said before, I'm not an entrepreneur, and people have explained to me I'm not a great business manager. So I turned over management of craigslist to a great team in 2000 and got out of the way. But they kept to the same values we all shared: that you can do well by doing good.

As Nacie makes clear in this book, one of the things that's going on is that jobs are changing in this economy, and she offers a lot of solid guidance on how to meet those challenges. That's a good thing, because one of the best things you can do for someone is give them a job, or help them get one.

I also like the title, since I'm a bird lover.

Craig Newmark
Founder of craigslist and craigconnects
San Francisco
December 2011

# THE FINCH EFFECT

# survival of the fittest

I am going to be honest with you: this is not a career book. This is not a book about how to polish your résumé—although we will touch on that. It is not a book about building your brand or refining your skills, even though we will explore both concepts in depth. Since we will work on changing your perspective, leveraging modern technology, and tapping into your entrepreneurial potential, you might think this book is about those topics. But it's not.

This is a book about something much larger. This is a book about professional evolution.

In 1831, Charles Darwin embarked on a five-year geological expedition on *HMS Beagle* around the world. While we all remember him as he was in his later years—a graying old man with an affinity for eccentric facial hair—at the time of the voyage he was just a 22-year-old university graduate who possessed an uncanny natural intelligence, a hunger for adventure, and a desire to see the world before he settled into his anticipated profession as a parson.

Young Charles was likely not so different from myself or other twenty-something college graduates: old enough to make his own choices, desperate to spread his wings and start really living, yet still inexperienced and naïve in ways he couldn't yet understand. In a letter to his friend and mentor, John Stevens Henslow, the man who would be Charles Darwin shared a thought that most of us can relate to: "I dare hardly look forward to the future, for I do not know what will become of me."[1] When he wanted to sign up as a volunteer on the voyage of the *Beagle* to help with the recording of geological findings, his father said what most of our fathers would likely say if we pitched the idea of being on a boat in strange waters for half a decade: "Are you out of your mind?"

I am paraphrasing. In his autobiography, Darwin noted that his father "strongly objected" and would only relent in his objections if someone sensible (read: not Darwin) said the trip was a good idea. Luckily Darwin's uncle, apparently a sensible man with a vicarious need for adventure, spoke up in favor of the plan, allowing the young lad to set off and experience what Darwin reflected on later as "the most important event of my life."

The voyage also turned out to be one of the most important events in the history of modern science thanks in part to observations Darwin made while the *Beagle* was stopped at the wild Galápagos Islands. Located west of Ecuador, the volcanic archipelago was positively simmering with fresh deposits of lava and such a diverse array of giant tortoises, iguanas, and unusual vegetation that Robert FitzRoy, the captain of the ship, deemed the shore "fit for pandemonium."[2]

While documenting and recording the diverse array of wildlife on the islands, Darwin noticed the finches—small, plainly colored, and all-around unimposing birds that occurred in large flocks across the archipelago. He soon conceded to "inexplicable confusion" over classifying the birds. Though there seemed to be variations in size and shape and other physical features, they surprisingly had similar feeding habits and plumage, which led a perplexed Darwin to dub them "very curious."[3]

By the time the *Beagle* set sail for its next call, Tahiti, Darwin had added six types of finches to his specimen menagerie. It wasn't until 1837, two years after his visit to the archipelago, that Darwin—with a little help from some scientist friends—realized his Galápagos finch samples weren't just different types but entirely different species of bird. Upon further examination he discovered that these unique species of finches had done something extraordinary: within a few generations, the beaks of the birds had altered rapidly in both size and shape to accommodate changes in their food sources and environment. Furthermore, each of the islands in the Galápagos had its own distinct set of finch species. Darwin theorized that the different species likely came from one common ancestor yet had all adapted over time to their present environments. In the process, they had become completely different birds.

This observation planted the seed for his theory of evolution, though it would take Darwin over twenty more years to fully articulate and present that theory to the world in his 1859 book, *On the Origin of Species*. For those of you who skipped out on high school biology, I can recap one of the book's paradigm-shattering messages in one simple phrase: *survival of the fittest*.

We've all heard about the survival of the fittest, and I am willing to bet that if asked to summarize it you would say something like "kill or be killed" or "only the strong will survive." But the truth is that through his work with the finches, Darwin understood that "the fittest" were not necessarily the most aggressive or dominant of any species but those most able to adapt to changes in their environment.

Nearly two hundred years ago, Darwin's seminal work was informed by the finches' prodigious ability to adapt. But for us modern professionals, the example they provide—of rapid adaptation and survival—is more than just a scientific principle: it gives us insight into how to move forward and succeed in a job market that, right before our eyes, is shifting away from the decades-old nine-to-five standard into something yet undefined and still forming. The collision of chronically high unemployment with an expanding global workforce (among other factors) has turned the American job market into an ongoing survival-of-the-fittest scenario where professionals have a clear choice: evolve their careers or risk career extinction.

To be sure, this isn't the first time in American history when the job market has been dicey. The last century featured the Great Depression of the 1930s as well as recessions at the end of the 1940s and in the early 1970s. We've also had several notable recent recessions—in the early 1980s (which saw unemployment peak at 10.8 percent), in 1991 (6.9 percent), and in the early 2000s (6.0 percent).[4] Each of these periods brought its own challenges, including job market crises of varying degrees, and each one called upon the workers of the day to evolve in order to survive.

Yet many economists argue that the job market we find ourselves in today is more severe than any of those mentioned above, except the Great Depression. At the time I am writing this, the national unemployment rate isn't as horrific as 1982's peak unemployment. But our recovery from recession has been slower. As a July 2011 *Wall Street Journal* article notes, "The economy's improvement since the recession's end in June 2009 has been the worst, or one of the worst, since the government started tracking these trends after World War II."[5] And there's a twist: when recovery comes, there's no guarantee the job market will look like it did before. In fact, as we'll discuss in just a page or two, there are many signs that it will look quite different.

In this unsettled, challenging time, when the applicant-to-job ratio hovers at 5:1, I would identify two kinds of professionals:

- those who are treading water (at best), waiting for the job market to recover from this latest recession
- those who are advancing their careers and helping to shape the job market of tomorrow, in spite of the challenges

The first group, which comprises millions of displaced and distraught Americans, still believes in the safety of the traditional nine-to-five job market. This belief makes them an endangered species. The second group, which I have come to dub "the Fittest," has read the writing on the wall and understands that the traditional employment structure is probably going the way of the dinosaur—but faster. Instead of waiting for a recovery in the job market that is never going to come— at least not in the form most people imagine—the Fittest are taking their own career fates in hand. They are using a set of five strategies, which I call "the Finch Effect" (in honor of

Darwin's avian inspirations), to evolve their careers so that they can not only survive changes in the job market but thrive in them.

As humans, one of our main evolutionary advantages is that we can adapt to changes in our lifetime, learning from and teaching each other to accelerate our adaptation. And we use this strength to keep honing our strategies as our environment changes. So a brilliant feature of the Finch Effect is that its strategies are teachable and replicable: once you know them, you can use them to adapt to any change in the job market, from current circumstances to those that will arise in the future.

But before you can make the most of these strategies, you need to make peace with one of the main changes in the current business environment: the age of the nine-to-five worker is over.

## the end of an era

While politicians desperately point to little sparkles in the darkness to try to convince the populace that the traditional full-time job market is improving, career experts and economists around the world are starting to come to a shocking consensus: the job market that is emerging from the recession is fundamentally different from the one that crumbled under our feet just a few years ago. This new, emerging market is global and technologically driven, and it is not *employee* based but rather, *contractor* based.[6]

Companies of all sizes across the country are rethinking the very nature of employment. Instead of hiring workers in a traditional full-time-with-benefits format, many are moving toward nontraditional labor arrangements, such as using independent contractors and breaking full-time positions into several part-time jobs to reduce costs.

Translation: the job market your father worked in, the one you studied your way through years of school to join, the one you have trained yourself to succeed in, is right in the middle of its swan song (or death rattle, depending on your perspective)—and no amount of government stimulus, tax restructuring, or fervent denial can revive it.

I would bet you have already witnessed the tell-tale signs of the demise of nine-to-five, though you might not have realized it:

- You notice that your company is starting to bring on more contract or part-time workers rather than traditional full-time employees
- Your siblings, friends, or children are graduating college, and instead of entering their chosen field in a permanent, full-time job, they find themselves working odd, part-time, or temporary jobs until "something opens up"
- In spite of your work experience and great recommendations, you are struggling to secure an in-person interview, let alone a job offer

If you are looking for someone or something to blame for the end of the job market as we know it, you can point an enraged finger at simple math: in a traumatized economy, the cost-to-benefit ratio of maintaining a full-time, salaried workforce is no longer earning out. When a company hires a full-time employee, it is paying more than just a salary; it is also responsible for a bevy of benefits and taxes. In addition to compensation, an employer must pay a portion of each employee's Social Security and Medicare taxes, as well as an unemployment tax and additional state taxes. Employers of full-time workers have traditionally been expected to provide a benefits package, including costly perks such as healthcare insurance, paid sick days, and paid vacation.

In good economic times, these costs are grudgingly accepted. But in an economy like we've experienced over the last few years, they can quickly add up to more than a business can handle.

To compete—or even just to keep their doors open—many organizations have replaced many members of their full-time workforce with a variety of nontraditional workers (independent contractors, freelancers, temporary workers), keeping a much smaller core of in-house, full-time employees in certain key positions. For example, a September 2011 article in the *Boston Globe* noted that the number of part-time workers in Massachusetts increased by 18 percent from January to August 2011, reflecting a reluctance among businesses to offer full-time positions during the flagging economic recovery. What business owners in Massachusetts and elsewhere have found is that nontraditional workers have met and exceeded job requirement expectations while keeping overhead low. The success of the nontraditional model is reflected in the fact that (according to the almost one thousand CFO respondents to the 2010 Duke/CFO Magazine Global Business Outlook survey) one fourth of recent new hires have been contract or temporary workers. Conversely, respondents expected full-time hiring to increase by less than one percentage point in the next year.[7]

Another strategy organizations of all sizes are using to reduce overhead is outsourcing tasks to the global labor market.

Over the last ten years, major multinational American companies, who employ about a fifth of the United States workforce, have sent 2.4 million jobs overseas to emerging labor markets like Brazil, China, and India. Brands like GE, Caterpillar, and Cisco are tapping into the globalized workforce to both expand their international clout and reduce their overhead. The consulting firm McKinsey & Company notes that a major airline carrier could save $100 million each year by sending jobs that don't require face-to-face interaction, like making reservations, overseas to cheaper labor markets. And those markets can be really cheap: the difference between hiring an overseas employee versus a US-based employee in the computer industry, for example, can be as much as $80,000 in salary commitments per year.[8]

But outsourcing is a strategy no longer reserved for massive corporations: small businesses, even microbusinesses, have the ability to tap into this global workforce to reduce overhead. Web-based services like eLance.com, Freelancer.com, and V-Teams connect even the smallest businesses and entrepreneurs with a global network of affordable professionals able to fill just about any gap, from call answering to market research to sales qualifying. In my years as a freelance writer and consultant, just about every small client I have worked with—from a start-up holistic health website to a boutique leadership development firm—outsources at least one of its administrative, technical, or research-related roles. You understand why outsourcing is an attractive option for even the smallest business when you notice that the hourly cost for firms in India, the Ukraine, and the United States to do the same work—including bookkeeping, content writing, and web design—is listed at $15, $20, and $85 by country, respectively, on eLance.

Think for a minute about what you as an American professional expect to make in an entry or midlevel position compared to these figures, and then think about how much of your desired job could be done remotely by someone in another country. It can be a shocking comparison. It's easy to see why, in the March 2010 edition of *Entrepreneur Magazine*, Bruce Judson, senior faculty fellow at the Yale School of Management, was quoted as advising business owners to "Outsource as much as possible."[9]

Some people will single out factors such as chronically high unemployment, or advancements in technology, or rising gas prices, or the global workforce, or bursting real estate bubbles, or healthcare costs as the main culprit in the demise of nine-to-five. But the truth is that *all* of these—and myriad other, smaller factors—have played a part in why career security no longer lives in the promise of the traditional full-time position. It now lives in the promise of the gig economy.

## the rise of the gig economy

Around the turn of the millennium, the term "gig economy" started cropping up in the work of economic analysts and job market experts to define a newly fashionable trend among professionals: piecing together multiple and unrelated projects, known as "gigs," rather than working in a full-time position for just one employer. Throughout the 2000s, the phrase and the work arrangement it described waxed and waned in popularity, until the recession brought it back into heavy use in many economic circles. In 2009, Tina Brown, editor in chief of TheDaily Beast.com, noted the resurgence of "gig economy," stating, "No one I know has a job anymore. They've got Gigs."[10]

What constitutes a "gig" can include everything from the unglamorous job of cleaning a gymnasium two nights a week to the incredibly fabulous role of consultant for a Fortune 500 corporation. Patching together a host of independent contracting, consulting, or freelancing positions to equal or exceed a full-time salary is the objective of gig employment. Brown points to a friend of hers who did PR for an airline magazine two days a week, provided consulting for another business three days a week, and also served as a business speaker for a tech company in his spare time. Brown notes that in a recent TheDailyBeast.com survey of employed Americans over 18, around one third of the five hundred people questioned used a gig structure and claimed to earn over $75,000 per year doing so.[11]

In all fairness, we were warned years ago that the nine-to-five job market was going to be replaced by a gig economy. We were told, however, that the shift to gigs would be our *choice*, not that it would be thrust upon us by a series of dramatic economic events.

In his 2001 book *Free Agent Nation*, Daniel Pink predicted that the era of the "Organization Man"—a term that Pink notes was originally coined by *Fortune* magazine editor William H. Whyte in 1956 to mean a person who spent his entire career moving up the ladder in a handful of companies—was coming to an end thanks to a boom in the American worker's desire to be self-employed. He believed that things like the internet, cell phones, and a now archaic phenomenon known as WebTV would inspire Americans to go rogue and leave the nine-to-five, causing the traditional work structure's ultimate demise. Pink foresaw a workforce of happy freelancers who had voluntarily broken off with the full-time employee model, forcing its extinction.[12]

Though the early and mid-2000s did see a slight rise in freelancers and start-ups, it also saw a serious inflation of salaries and benefits offered by companies competing desperately with one another for top talent. The result was that the American workforce didn't, as Pink suggested, walk away from the traditional job market; instead, we flocked to it in droves and were absolutely sideswiped when suddenly the full-time employee model started buckling underneath us at the start of the recession.

But where the nine-to-five model failed in a recession-wracked America, the gig-centric model quietly succeeded—driven not by the choices of workers but by the needs of business. The gig economy has allowed businesses to stay open by creatively dividing a huge amount of work and responsibility across part-time and contract workers.

And here is where the major split occurs between the Fittest and the rest of the workforce: instead of waiting for the job market to return to the status quo of the mid-2000s, the Fittest have adopted a "gig mindset" that allows them to adapt and flourish whether they choose to remain in traditional jobs or embrace nontraditional opportunities. This mindset places power in the hands of the individual professional—not ceding it all to the organization—thus increasing both emotional and vocational resilience. So while the rest of us feel ourselves at the mercy of employers to decide our fate (Will we be laid off? Will our pay be reduced?), the Fittest are surviving, thriving, and setting the trends for the emerging job market.

Don't let the phrase "gig mindset" fool you. This approach is meant not only for freelancers or future freelancers; it can be successfully adopted by any professional in any industry and any job structure who wants to keep the stability of a career in hand. Adopting the gig mindset is so crucial to your adaptive success that we will continue to explore it throughout the book—in fact, it constitutes the first strategy of the Finch Effect.

## the search for a way forward

Five years ago I still believed in the security of the traditional job market just like everyone else. Months before college graduation I had a job lined up in the financial software industry and was positively starry-eyed over the entry-level salary and elaborate benefits package that came with my first grown-up job. But the thrills of direct-deposit paychecks and casual Fridays soon lost their luster, and I was left with a long commute to a job that didn't call for the use of my natural skills or passions. In September 2008, one week before Lehman Brothers collapsed, I decided to go rogue and quit my supposedly safe nine-to-five job to pursue a writing career in professional development.

My friends and family were all concerned that I had made a mistake giving up a stable paycheck and secure job to take on a career that, in the first few years, proved to be mostly freelance-based. However, thanks to a set of great clients and online writing outlets, I landed on my feet and settled into my new career with little issue, in spite of the recession that was steadily gaining strength.

But as recession-plagued 2008 turned into an even bleaker 2009, I started to notice that many of those who had advised me on the safety of the traditional job market were finding themselves unemployed, underemployed, or living under near constant threats of layoffs. One of my best friends lost her job at a large accounting firm; a speaking circuit a family member was scheduled to do was canceled; and several of my college friends found themselves waiting tables or landscaping because jobs had dried up in their industries. What really struck me was that it wasn't just one group that was suffering. My friends and family, across generations and industries, all suddenly had something in common: the bottom had fallen out from under them, and they had no idea what to do next.

I felt like I had dodged a bullet by making my career transition when I did. As I observed the struggles of those around me, I found myself wracked with something akin to survivor's guilt: why should things be working out for me while those I cared for felt so powerless and lost?

My guilt was transformed into a desire to find a solution after I visited my younger brother at college. He and I have always been close friends; I don't believe any sister could ask for a better brother. The college he attended was only a few hours from where I lived, so I drove out a few times a semester to take him to lunch and catch up. It was April, and I had come up for the final lunch visit before the year was over. We were just digging into a gigantic plate of nachos at the local pub when he suddenly went quiet. When I asked him what was wrong, he told me that only one of his seven graduating friends had been able to find a job, and the job was working for his dad's construction company. "I don't understand, Nace—they had internships and got their degrees. They did everything right. What's going to happen to them? What's going to happen to me when I graduate?"

He frowned for another moment before refocusing his attention on the nachos and redirecting the conversation back to lighter topics. But as I drove home that afternoon, I couldn't stop thinking about how crazy it all seemed. Just two years earlier, the goal for any new graduate wasn't only to find a job; it was to find the *highest paying* job. Now there were no jobs in sight, and the future that had once looked so rosy for me and my friends looked uncertain and confusing for my brother.

There had to be a solution, a way forward, not only for him but also for my friends, family, and even myself. I had been lucky with my work so far—in fact, I had just started working with a boutique professional development firm as their director of learning and development. But I was becoming aware that career security was not something to be taken for granted. Who knew when the rug might be pulled out from under me as well? There had to be some people out there who had found a way to keep their careers advancing in spite of the changes in the job market. And I decided that I was going to find out who they were and how they were doing it.

I have spent the last two years of my life doing just that. In that time, I have met and spoken with professionals from all walks of life, in every corner of this country, and in all career stages. You will meet several of them over the course of this book. I have talked with economic experts, job market gurus, human resource consultants, and even a few celebrities in my quest to understand how we—modern professionals—can continue to move our careers and lives forward in the face of volatile work conditions and unstable job markets. And what I have learned has brought me from a glimpse of the not-too-distant future all the way back to the work of a 150-year-dead evolutionary naturalist, and a little tropical bird.

I am happy to report that my quest has been a success: there is a way forward, and it is accessible to all. What struck me was that the professionals who are not just surviving but also thriving in the current job climate—members of the Fittest—all share a set of strategies in common, in spite of their diverse industries and backgrounds. While I would love to lay claim to the brilliance of these strategies, I insist that I am not their creator, just their reporter. The five strategies that make up the Finch Effect are drawn from the experiences and insights of professionals around the country and are presented in this book in the hope that you can implement them for your own success. While each of these strategies can stand on its own as a valuable step in improving your work life in any economy, I have organized them as a sequence in order to provide the most impact. Each strategy builds off the one that came before it. I recommend that you read this book, and complete the exercises it contains, in sequential order to get the most benefit out of each chapter. Here are the five Finch Effect strategies:

1. *Adopt a gig mindset.* Focus on shifting your current perspective and expectations for your professional future to match the shifts in the job market. The Fittest have stopped waiting around for the job market to "go back to normal" and are instead reframing their perspectives to create new (and more interesting) career ladders.

    This strategy explores the concept of the gig mindset, and how members of the Fittest are taking a page from the freelancer's book to stay adaptable to change and remain in control of their careers. Once you make the mental shift to taking ownership of your career path, you are in a position to actually *do* something about it, regardless of what's happening in the job market.

2. *Identify your professional value.* Isolate, differentiate, and leverage what makes you stand out from other professionals.

Mom always told you that you were special and different from the other kids. Well, today is the day you are going to take Mom at her word and figure out exactly what makes you stand out from other professionals in your skills, presentation, experience, and career mission. Part of surviving (and then thriving) is picking out those skills that make you worth noticing. This second Finch Effect strategy focuses on developing your *adaptive professional brand* (APB)—a tool for organizing, communicating, and leveraging your professional value effectively.

3. *Cultivate your skills.* Here you take the skills you outlined in the second strategy and develop them to their highest potential. It's not going to be enough to just talk (or tweet) a big game about how distinctive you are from other professionals out there—you need to be able to back it up with serious skills. The third principle of the Finch Effect focuses on identifying what you need to do to get the skills that are central to your adaptive professional brand to their highest potential—whether they include crunching numbers or designing jewelry—and then making and implementing a plan to actually do it.

4. *Nurture your social network.* Learn to communicate and grow your adaptive professional brand through social media—or learn to do it better. The fourth Finch Effect principle focuses on optimizing your use of Facebook (and Twitter, and LinkedIn . . . ) to craft, package, and grow an individual professional brand fueled by social media. Your online profiles and website are the best places to start projecting your value proposition, which in turn helps you market yourself better to potential employers, clients, or customers. Get ready to start clicking, because we are

living in an online world and the Fittest are online girls (and boys).

5. *Harness your entrepreneurial energy.* Build entrepreneurial skills and tactics into your professional identity to optimize your position in the new job market. As the tide of the job market continues to shift away from the traditional full-time employee, you (and other savvy professionals) will need to rely more on your entrepreneurial energy to win jobs, establish new income streams, and build your value proposition. This final strategy of the Finch Effect reviews how other members of the Fittest have started building entrepreneurial systems and ventures into their professional identities, whether in their current jobs, through side businesses, or as part of a transition into full-fledged entrepreneurship.

At its core, the way forward that the Finch Effect outlines is the way of evolution. To me there is something comforting in the idea that our professional survival is rooted in such a timeless biological imperative. It is something we, as entities of this earth, are programmed down to our cells to do. What became clear to me as I started to compile these strategies based on how members of the Fittest thrive in this new world, is that a willingness to take ownership and responsibility for your own career is essential. If you take nothing else away from this book, I hope it is the idea that the future belongs to those who look to themselves and their own abilities for their security and success.

In fact, one of the most liberating things about this job market shift is that it allows each of us to redefine success in a way that is tailored to who we are as unique professionals and individuals. Almost all members of the Fittest I've met over the last few years have redefined success in their own image as part of their strategy for thriving. They recognize that as the rules of the game have changed, the prizes have as well.

In the traditional nine-to-five job market, your entire career was supposed to be an upward climb toward the three basic peaks: the highest salary, the most impressive job title, and the ability to improve your economic status (for example, living in a good neighborhood). Just a few years ago, owning a Hummer was considered a huge indicator of achievement and wealth. That one truck (or should I say tank?) was an embodiment of success: it was expensive to buy and keep and sent a clear message of your status in society to everyone within eyesight or earshot. Mike Tyson, Paris Hilton, and Arnold Schwarzenegger were all proud owners, and the brand was so synonymous with success that General Motors even made Hummer limos.

But in 2009, GM announced it was discontinuing the Hummer as part of its bankruptcy filing, making the brand just one more casualty of the recession. Today the Hummers that are left on the road are archaic reminders of a prerecession world that has gone extinct in just a few years due to rising gas prices, accelerating concerns over climate change, increasing cost-of-living expenses, and a hollowed-out economy.

Many traditional indicators of success are going the way of the Hummer. Private-college degrees, McMansions, and even the executive title are losing some degree of relevance. Just as the job market is shifting away from the traditional employee model, the Fittest are replacing conventional definitions of success with personal ones that not only adapt to support their evolving careers but also provide authentic, ongoing fulfillment.

Just ask Rob.

Before the housing bubble burst (and the rest of the economy came crashing down after it), 28-year-old Rob worked as a real estate agent in Nevada. He was good at his job and earned enough to pay off his car, buy a condo, and accumulate a fairly respectable wardrobe. Yet in spite of all these trapping of traditional success, Rob wasn't satisfied: "at that time, I felt that I was 'successful' according to the standards of others, yet looking back I realize how disconnected and empty I really felt." When the real estate market crashed, Rob had two choices: keep treading water doing what he was doing, or adapt his career to the changing job market. Rob chose to adapt.

Drawing from his business experience, Rob launched a one-person consulting firm in 2009 that provides marketing and brand solutions to small businesses around the country. Today his business is thriving, and his understanding of success has become personal in a way it never was before. "My perception of success has drastically shifted from being able to afford the nicest of everything to being able to help others build their business. When I can help independent, small businesses articulate their message and achieve results, I consider myself successful."

Just as he embraced evolution in his career, Rob has embraced an evolving definition of what success means to him and experienced a greater sense of fulfillment because of it. His personal definition of success will likely continue to change over time as his career continues to adapt to new opportunities and shifts in the market. Yet while Rob's perspective on success is his own, his method of identifying it is shared by all members of the Fittest: he specifically defines it as something actionable.

One of the downsides of leading a trend is that those on the vanguard are faced with an overwhelming array of choices and possibilities. While having myriad opportunities can be exciting and intoxicating, it can also cause indecision, self-doubt, and analysis paralysis. It is no different when trailblazing your own personal definition of success.

To manage this potentially engulfing power of possibility, the Fittest define success through actionable and achievable goals. These goals create a renewing and regular source of achievement and fulfillment, which in turn provides motivation, professional prowess, and more success. This cycle allows the Fittest to subtly shape their definition of success to adapt to the ever-changing market landscape.

Consider Rob. Today he defines success in part by helping his clients find their brand's voice. Every time he works with a new client—which occurs often throughout the year—he has an opportunity to experience success by his definition. Each time he succeeds by his definition, he reinforces his professional confidence and motivation and becomes a more capable, experienced, and attractive prospect for future clients. Additionally, should future shifts in the market require him to do something different for his clients, he can easily adapt his personal definition of success to reflect it. As we've seen, traditional definitions of success aren't always as adaptable to changing environments (sorry, Hummer).

This strategy of defining and engendering success through achievable goals, natural to many of the Fittest, is also supported by psychological research on achievement, which has consistently concluded that clearly defined goals focus attention, motivate effort, encourage persistence, and facilitate the identification or creation of strategies to accomplish the objective.[13]

Ironically, when it comes to defining personal success and establishing clear career goals, most of us are working against ourselves. In the present economy, where it feels like all choice has been taken away from us, we find it hard to purposely eliminate options and close doors. We want to "keep our options open" and "see what happens."

Yet this unwillingness to close doors and make exclusive choices leads to only one thing: an endangered vocational existence marked by treading water with everyone else who is waiting for the job market to improve. If you want to join the Fittest and define success by your own goals, you need to get comfortable setting your own standards and goals, and achieving them.

## break it down: your definition of personal success

As you begin your journey toward becoming a member of the Fittest, you should start to think about what your conception of personal success in the new job market will be. I recommend you keep in mind only two basic principles of personal success as you start to craft your own definition:

1. Your personal definition of success can be as simple or as complex as you want . . .
2. . . . as long as all elements are *actionable* and *achievable* within a reasonable time frame

The one other suggestion I can share with you is to stay away from the verbs "to be" or "to have" when thinking about your definition. I've always found goals and visions of success that include those verbs to be ultranebulous; they are also usually reminiscent of the traditional pinnacles of success, like "My goal is to *have* a million dollars!" or "I will *be* successful when I am an EVP!" These definitions aren't going to get you very far, because there is no sense of time or identifiable action for how they will happen.

Your definition of personal success could be as short and sweet as "Success to me means opening my pastry shop in the next eighteen months," or it could be as long as an entire page. You can use whatever language you find easy to remember and hold onto. It can be something you needlepoint on a pillow or keep totally to yourself. It's an open canvas of potential on which you can form your own watchword. There are as many definitions of personal success as there are members of the Fittest. That's why it's called personal success.

If your definition of personal success doesn't immediately stand out to you, I encourage you to use any or all of the following prompts to jump-start your thought process:

- What reputation would you like to have among your colleagues, competitors, or customers? What accomplishments would earn that reputation?
- Which elements of your value proposition are you most proud of? How can you leverage them more effectively?
- What skills do you need to master to do your type of work most effectively?
- Think of one or two people you admire in your field—mentors or leaders. What do you most admire about them? What skills or knowledge do they have that you admire? How did they achieve their position?
- What is currently out there (either online, as a service, or as a product) that you think is a good idea but could be done much better? What's wrong with the current version, and how could it be improved?

## the unexpected opportunity of vocational darwinism

One of the most ironic things about humans is that although we are programmed for evolution—just like the finches—we often find the process of change uncomfortable and scary. Then we dig in our heels, shut our eyes tight, and hope that whatever is being asked of us can be avoided or will just go away.

The business-model transformation we are experiencing right now cannot be avoided and will not go away, no matter how much we try to soothe each other into thinking things are getting better (translate: "back to the way they were before the recession"). We need to face it head-on and with an open mind, or be steamrolled and left flat in the dust.

Not all elements of this transformation—or other, future transformations—have to be uncomfortable or scary; in fact, when you get past the end-of-careers-as-we-know-them part, the change is actually full of potential and opportunity. The future of the workforce is still undefined and lawless. The rules of the game will be decided by whoever strikes out from the masses first and sets the tone; those who follow will copy the examples of the initial trendsetters. You can be one of those setting the trends.

You are in a perfect position to define what the future of the workforce looks like and to lead this vocational transformation. Why spend time and effort trying to stay on the sinking ship that is the full-time employee model? You can use this opportunity to forge a new path toward long-term financial security, a real work-life balance, and vocational victory.

And that is what this book is all about. In the coming chapters, we are going to examine and explore each of the five strategies—adopt a gig mindset, identify your value, cultivate your skills, nurture your social network, and harness your entrepreneurial energy—in detail, break down how to put them in action, and meet some members of the Fittest who have used them to thrive. By the end of this book, you'll be ready to tackle the ups and downs of not only this job market but also any other job market that comes our way—because there will be other shifts, other recessions, and other good times that ask us to reevaluate how we operate within the job market and how we can continue to succeed.

To get the most out of this book, you will need to proceed with two thoughts in mind: "I am capable of making these changes," and "I am committed to making these changes." You may not fully understand how you are going to change over the course of this book, but you need to start on this journey of professional evolution with confidence in your ability to actually change. There are so many people in the world who believe they are who they are and that's all they'll ever be. If that statement resonates with you, I want you to read the following words carefully: As a being on this planet, you were not only born capable of growing and changing but born with the biological *imperative* to grow and change. Very little separates you from the finches when it comes to the capacity to change (except perhaps a few feathers here and there). So please repeat this sentence to yourself: "I am capable of making these changes."

Additionally, you need to be willing to commit to the changes this book asks you to make. Change in itself is hard, but without the commitment to sustain and maintain it, you are wasting your time. This book will ask you to dig deep and go outside of your comfort zone to see your career and potential in new and different ways. If you are not ready to commit to and work through the strategies to their fullest capacity, then I recommend you find a different career book to skim through.

If you are ready for the change and commitment that these strategies will call on you to make, then you are ready to begin. As you start working through the first strategy, remember that you are in good company. All of us, whether we have been in the workforce for decades or are peering into an uncertain future from university halls, are facing the same job market with the same challenges. And all of us have the potential to be members of the Fittest.

Are you ready to be one of the Fittest?

I say yes.

# 2

# adopt a gig mindset

She never expected it would happen to her.

After almost two years at one of the Big Four accounting firms, Renee found herself on the receiving end of a pink slip.

Losing your job was hardly unique in April 2009, and Renee wasn't the first of her friends to be out of a job since the recession started. All of the Big Four firms—which include PricewaterhouseCoopers, Ernst and Young, Deloitte, and KPMG—were instituting massive layoffs to keep afloat in the poor economy.

But for Renee, the pink slip was more than just a notice of dismissal—it was the end of real job security. "I went into accounting thinking it was going to be a stable career for me, that it was a smart move and I'd always have a job. I thought I would work at my company for a long time and work my way up the ladder. When I found out they were laying me off, all that security and plan for the future just evaporated."

It was hard to believe that just three years earlier she had felt so invincible in her career. After finishing a summer internship with the firm, Renee had been offered a job there in September of her senior year in college. "I felt very proud, because it was a prestigious company and I had a job before most people even knew what they wanted to do. I felt like it was an accomplishment, and knowing there was a really nice salary and signing bonus waiting for me after graduation allowed me to relax a little my senior year."

By April 2009, that salary, signing bonus, benefits package, and clear career ladder had been replaced with unemployment checks and a sense of hopelessness. Her new full-time job became searching for employment, sending out applications, and researching companies. In October 2009, after six months out of work, Renee found an entry-level position at a small accounting firm. She expected that since she had a job again things would go back to normal and she would get back on the path she had started on at her first firm. Within a few months, her expectations had changed.

"It became clear to me that the career path that I had started to pursue at that accounting firm was gone. Or at least it was becoming less of a sure thing. Everyone at my new firm was holding onto their jobs for dear life—especially those with twenty to thirty years of experience under their belt. They weren't risking a move onwards or upwards, and that lack of mobility trickled down to everyone else."

After talking with friends across various industries, Renee realized that movement up the career ladder—which just two years earlier had felt steady and predictable, more like an escalator—had been universally halted. When it would restart was anyone's guess, but by the look of things she was predicting it wouldn't be anytime soon. In light of her stalled career, Renee had two choices: tread water and wait for things to start moving again, however long that took; or take ownership of her own career ladder and adapt to the new norm.

She chose to adapt.

"I realized that I had to think about my position as a way to build my skill set and add to my résumé, even though it didn't offer much in the way of moving up the ladder."

She brought that attitude with her when in the summer of 2010 she changed jobs again—this time voluntarily—to take a sales training position at a biotechnology company. "I wanted to continue to broaden my skill base outside of the accounting world and try something different."

Renee still works at the biotechnology firm, but she knows that's not her final career destination. To keep her options open and her résumé growing, Renee recently earned her Certified Public Accountant license and has started providing financial planning services to a small clientele in her free time. Instead of having a clear-cut career path through a large corporation, the future feels open and unknown. But that's just fine with her. "Being laid off was one of the best things that happened to my career. It taught me how much power I didn't think I had in my hands and forced me to retake control of its direction."

Now she is focusing on developing and deepening her skill set by taking additional accounting classes, and on identifying her professional brand (two of the Finch Effect principles we'll visit in later chapters). When asked what her biggest takeaway was from the past four years of her career journey, Renee kept her answer short: "That career stability, and even your career ladder, comes from you, not a company."

Over the last few years, I have had the privilege to meet and speak with some amazing people—like Renee—around the country, who are not letting this precarious job market get the best of them or their careers. I've connected with jewelry makers in Arizona, lawyers in Kansas, and nurses in Vermont. I've spoken to writers and web developers and consultants across myriad industries and learned a valuable secret: professionals who are moving their careers forward—the members of the Fittest—are letting go of the career expectations that accompanied the traditional nine-to-five model. Instead, they are creating their own career security and embracing new career ladders. They have adopted the *gig mindset.*

In the previous chapter, I introduced the concept of the gig mindset and talked about how members of the Fittest are taking a page from the freelancer's book to stay adaptable to change and remain in control. This first of the five strategies of the Finch Effect involves cultivating that mindset and adopting an action-oriented mental framework through which to view and implement the other Finch Effect strategies.

But what exactly is the gig mindset? It's the ability to see yourself as an empowered professional, not only capable of but interested in pursuing various and complementary career opportunities to enhance your vocational success. While the concept draws on the imagery of cobbling together different "gigs" to make a full-time position, the mindset is really about taking ownership of your career and being open to change so that you can effectively weather any economic climate.

I can tell you that the years I spent freelance writing changed how I look at the nature of working. That period instilled in me the concept of ownership for my career; whether I succeeded or failed as a freelancer was based less on my clients than on my own choices, discipline, and openness to opportunity. When I left freelancing behind to work with a professional development company, I took that sense of career ownership with me. I was amazed at how different I felt compared to my first sojourn in full-time employment, years earlier. One of the main reasons I yearned for the freelance life to begin with was that I felt so helpless in my first corporate job: at any point major decisions about my career could be made without my control—and what could I do about it? Nothing. I was lucky with the company I worked for, but I had friends who had to switch departments, give up key accounts, and even relocate without much say in the matter. And of course we all know the control an employer has over whether we even have the job. As far as I am concerned, that state of constant powerlessness about one of the largest aspects of life is no way to live, in any kind of economy.

But what I've found since reentering the employer-based workforce is that career ownership—the sense that you are in the driver's seat of your work life—has nothing to do with where you are working, whom you are working for, or what you are doing. It comes from something less tangible: accepting and embracing that your professional power and stability, as Renee so eloquently put it, "comes from you, not a company." This phrase is the real essence of the gig mindset, and we are going to spend the rest of this chapter cultivating it.

You may have noticed that the active verb in the definition of the gig mindset is *see*, not *do*. This is because when it comes to professional evolution, 90 percent of the likelihood of success springs from perspective, not action.

Each of us has a perspective that is individual and unique. It is shaped by countless factors, such as upbringing, experiences, and education, and it shifts throughout our life. Our perspective is an essential element of our evolution—professional or otherwise—because it reflects our interpretation of the world and our place in it. On the most basic, biological level it is meant to influence us to self-preserving actions: we perceive dark caves (or today, dark alleys) as dangerous and thus are compelled to avoid them; we perceive those around us as meaning us well or meaning us harm and are compelled to act accordingly, with welcome or caution; and we perceive the current job market as uncertain and unstable, so we are compelled to act conservatively and sit tight instead of professionally branching out and exploring.

There is no getting around it: our perspectives on situations and ourselves at any given moment heavily dictate what actions we take. I say that the success of career evolution is 90 percent dependent on perspective and 10 percent on action, but perhaps the ratio is skewed to an even greater extreme, such as 95 to 5 percent. This is why it is essential to get your perspective straight before initiating action strategies, and this is why we begin our exploration of the Finch Effect with the gig mindset.

As a strategy, adopting a gig mindset may be deceptively simple. You just decide that you want to adopt a more independent perspective on your career and go from there, right?

Wrong.

The human brain, for all its capabilities, does not function purely on logic, reason, or factual deduction. Instead, our thought processes are spaghetti-bowl messes of logic, reason, and deduction mixed with emotion, experience, expectations, and exaggeration, underlain by instinct. While these more colorful elements of our thinking are part of being human, they can cloud our ability to see the forest for the trees—or in this case, the ability to see the reality of a changed job market for our career expectations.

There is no doubt that our national experience during the recent recession and weak recovery has been a traumatic one. While economists have noted that a host of signs warned of such a downfall, it is safe to say that for most of us the financial collapse in September 2008 came as a shock, and a big one at that. It messed with our sense of security and national character, leaving us in a countrywide crisis over who we are as a people, where we are going, and what promises the Land of the Free can now make about opportunity.

Though the initial shock has worn off, we are still left with a pervasive sense of uncertainty. Will things recover and go back to normal, or is *this* the new norm? And if it is the new norm, how do we move forward by it?

The daily—scratch that—the *hourly* media bombardment we are subjected to doesn't answer that question; instead, I would argue that it clouds our ability to come to terms with the answer by sustaining a hope in a recovery that won't happen in the way we expect it to. It's not that we aren't intelligent or talented enough to understand that—quite the opposite. It's that psychological forces are at work (we'll get to those in a minute) that make restructuring your conception of your professional future a more challenging task than just flipping a switch.

The good news is that you can pave the way to a gig mindset by using a few simple tactics to build your resilience. These tactics can help you not only accept current and potential changes in your career but embrace them for what they really are: opportunities to truly be the master of your vocational fate and captain of your career-minded soul.

But before we turn to these tactics, let's take a closer look at one of the most powerful psychological forces that stand in our way of making this transition in perspective: confirmation bias.

## the limiting perspective of confirmation bias

Have you ever met someone who thinks his or her alma mater is the be-all and end-all in higher education?

I know I have—in fact, I am one of those people.

They always seem to know the latest statistic that supports how fabulous their college is. For example, Holy Cross—my alma mater—was ranked number 27 on the 2011 *Forbes* list of top colleges. These people always seem to be oddly ignorant about the less flattering aspects of their school. Obviously this doesn't apply to HC, but hypothetical examples include problems with grade inflation, unfair employment practices, and so on. You can tell such a person a really unsavory story about their school (what happened at an off-campus party?), and it seems to go in one ear and out the other. All the facts in the world won't change their steadfast belief that their school is the best, much to the exasperation of anyone who sees it differently. . . . Go HC!

See what I mean?

You might call this tunnel vision, but psychologists call it *confirmation bias*. Confirmation bias can be defined as a tendency for people to interpret information in ways that confirm their already established beliefs or preconceptions. We do this by homing in on supportive data and filtering out, dismissing, or arguing against the validity of any data that don't support those beliefs or preconceptions. This can happen consciously or unconsciously, but it does happen, often and powerfully. A review of studies on

confirmation bias—which featured nearly eight thousand participants in total—revealed that "people are twice as likely to seek
information that confirms what they already believe as they are
to consider evidence that would challenge those beliefs."[1]

I gave an example of confirmation bias influencing our
thinking on something lighthearted, school spirit. However, we
experience confirmation bias in our understanding of most
things, from religion to politics to relationships and—you
might have guessed it—our careers and the economy.

This can be a big problem, because when it comes to the
American job market, many of us have a strong belief that it is
going to go back to "normal." We've been raised to believe in
the strength and might of America as a global economic super-
power, and history has taught us that we always pull our way
back to some sense of normalcy out of down periods. We have
also been taught that if we do our part—go to school, get good
grades, work hard, and pay our dues—then, quid pro quo,
there will be a place for us in the traditional job market, where
salaries, benefits, paid vacations, and golden watches are all
part of the package. We may change career paths, but if we've
fulfilled our part of the bargain, we always expect that should
we want it, a place of security will be available to us.

Yet in this age of vocational Darwinism, where everything
is in flux, such beliefs can work strongly against us if instead of
changing with the times, we sit and wait for the current job
market "phase" to end. Our confirmation bias toward this
belief—that things will go back to our expectation of normal—
can work against our natural, basic evolutionary instincts to
adapt to change. If career evolution is 90 percent dependent on
perception and 10 percent on action, then having a confirmation bias that supports the recovery of the prerecession job

market will make it impossible for us to take appropriate adaptive action to thrive in the job market of tomorrow.

Why does our brain allow such warps in our perception to occur? Isn't perception supposed to be a psychological mechanism of self-protection? Scott Lilienfield, a psychologist at Emory University explained to the *Wall Street Journal* that confirmation bias occurs because "We're all mentally lazy. It's simply easier to focus our attention on data that supports our hypothesis, rather than to seek out evidence that might disprove it."[2]

But in defense of our "mental laziness," confirmation bias likely originated as a way for our brains to efficiently catalogue the huge amount of data it is bombarded with constantly. It can also help us subconsciously to protect ourselves from information that could prove stressful or provoke anxiety. Let's be honest: when it comes to our career future, it is definitely less stressful to think that things will return to a normal we already know rather than that they are changing into something unknown.

Yet when you come down to it, what separates members of the Fittest from everyone else is not intelligence. Or education. Or career experience. What separates members of the Fittest from all the other professionals out there is their willingness to look beyond such perspective-warping psychological mechanisms (even those with their best interests at heart) and allow themselves to be open to change and the opportunities to evolve.

## preparing for the gig mindset with resilience tactics

Yet this openness to change can be a tall order, especially when we are conscious of how many things are outside of our control, like the job market and the future of the economy. Why would you want to interject more chaos into that scenario by purposely inflicting change upon yourself?

The short answer is a refrain that you are starting to be very familiar with: change will happen, and is happening, with or without your consent. It is in your best interest to work with and potentially influence the change; otherwise, you risk losing even more control over your future—and losing out to those who are willing to step up to the plate.

One of the best ways to increase your openness to change and prepare yourself for a gig mindset is by building up your psychological resilience. The American Psychological Association (APA) defines resilience as "the process of adapting well in the face of adversity, trauma, tragedy, threats, or even significant sources of stress. It means 'bouncing back' from difficult experiences." In its extended definition of resilience, the APA notes that resilience can help us deal with challenging experiences like job loss, stress in the workplace, or financial concerns. For members of the Fittest, psychological resilience is a foundational element of their ability to thrive in spite of job market challenges. Resilience allows them to maintain an adaptive and action-focused perspective.[3]

Importantly, upping your resilience will not make you immune to the uncomfortable emotions associated with change—emotions like stress, anxiety, and a sense of upheaval. What improving your resilience will do is help you reduce stress and anxiety by coping with these emotions in more productive and proactive ways. So when I start to feel stressed about my future job prospects, my improved resilience skills help me avoid eating a pint of Chunky Monkey, and instead help me to use that anxious energy toward working on my professional brand (in theory, at least!).

The good news about resilience is that all of us already have it to one degree or another. The even better news is that you can continue to build up your own psychological resilience through a variety of mental tactics. The APA suggests ten main ways to increase one's resilience capacity; I have observed members of the Fittest using three of them as they worked to adopt the gig mindset:

- Avoid seeing crises as insurmountable problems
- Accept that change is part of living
- Maintain a hopeful outlook

Let's take a look at what each one of these tactics means in the context of your professional evolution and go over a few techniques to boost your resilience.

### Avoid Seeing Crises as Insurmountable

The first resilience tactic that can help you adopt the gig mindset is to "avoid seeing crises as insurmountable problems." For our purposes, you can imagine a crisis as being laid off, being unable to find employment, or being chronically underemployed. I'll admit that this tactic is easier spoken of than practiced when your livelihood is on the line. But this resilience tactic is crucial to maintaining an accurate and action-worthy perspective. As the APA notes, "you can't change the fact that highly stressful events happen, but you can change how you interpret and respond to these events."[4]

One of the best ways to put this tactic into practice and bring some perspective to crises versus insurmountable problems is through *visualization*. Now the trick about visualization is that like most things worth doing, it is a skill that can take some time to develop. It can feel downright silly to walk yourself through the exercise I am about to share with you, but bear with the process and try to repeat it once a day for a week to get in the swing of things. If thinking about visualization as a tool to reframe insurmountable problems is too out-there for you, then just remind yourself that similar exercises have been scientifically shown to provide notable health benefits, like lower blood pressure, headache relief, and better digestion.[5]

## break it down: visualization

I want you to try this: take five minutes or so and go into a quiet room somewhere away from your family, roommates, television, and smartphone. Once you get good at this practice, you can even do it in an empty conference room or office at work.

1. Sit comfortably and close your eyes.
2. Take three deep breaths. Breathe in through your nose, filling your lungs, and hold the breath for a moment before letting the breath out slowly through your mouth.
3. Continuing to breathe in through your nose and out through your mouth in a consistent rhythm, bring to mind an image of someplace you have been before that made you feel calm, safe, and in control. It could be your mother's living room, the middle of the woods on an October day, or even a concert somewhere.
4. Try to feel yourself in that place down to the smallest details. What are the smells? What surrounds you? What noises are you hearing? What do you feel—the sun on your face? the large fibers of a shag carpet?
5. Once you have that place clearly in your mind's eye, ask yourself what it is about the place that makes you feel calm, safe,

or in control. Is it the presence of people you love? A sense of
possibility and opportunity? A connection to something
larger? Home in on the cause of that feeling and why you
chose that place.

6.  Once you have identified the cause of that feeling, I want you
    to visualize its power as a small, green marble on the ground
    in front of you. With your eyes still closed, imagine reaching
    down and picking that marble up. Feel the weight of it in your
    hand and the cool smoothness of its surface.

7.  Once you can clearly visualize how the marble looks and feels,
    you are going to imagine putting it in your pants pocket so that
    you can pull it out to help you deal with whatever challenges
    face you. Feel the weight of the marble in your pocket.

8.  If you are comfortable doing so, I recommend reaffirming to
    yourself (out loud or silently), "I have everything I need within
    reach to tackle and overcome [insert challenge]." Imagine
    placing your hand inside your pocket to feel the marble there,
    and then take three deep breaths and slowly open your eyes.

If nothing else, a visualization practice like this one can drop
your stress level from a 9 to a 4 for no other reason than the
focus on your breath. Part of successfully adopting a gig mindset
is bringing ownership and control of your career into your own
hands. When you feel like the world is throwing mountains in
front of you, then literally imagining doing just that—bringing
ownership and control of your career into your own hands—is
what you need to reclaim perspective and get back on track.

## Accept Change

And we all know that mountains will be thrown. This is reflected in the next resilience tactic, "Accept that change is a
part of living." I know that when change is happening to you it

can feel like the cold grip of fate has singled you out from the rest of us happy people for torment. But change, growth, and yes, evolution are the very nature of life—nothing stays the same, nothing is static. We need to realize that though this constant state of change can sometimes mean that things (jobs, opportunities, expected income) are taken away from us without our consent, at the same time new opportunities appear and we can act on them.

One way to build your resilience and be more accepting of change is through conscious gratitude. In a down economy, you don't hear many people saying thank-you for things— especially things they have lost, like jobs, promotions, or clients. But studies have shown that taking time to acknowledge and express gratitude for positive things in your life can improve your ability to adapt in stressful situations, including anxiety-provoking career situations.[6] Here's an exercise I try to do on a daily basis (emphasis on "try"!) as I am drifting off to sleep. I find it is not only more effective than counting sheep but also an easy way to reframe my feelings about change in my life, particularly unwelcome change. You can do the entire exercise mentally like I do or write it down. If you are out like a light at night, then I recommend doing it when you are brushing your teeth or driving.

When it comes to using gratitude to help build your psychological resilience, more is more. Research has confirmed that the more you feel grateful for, and the more you acknowledge that gratitude, the greater resilience benefit you'll get from the practice. So don't be afraid to include in your gratitude list everything from the man who held the elevator door for you this morning to that gorgeous sunset. It's all bringing you one step closer to effectively adopting your gig mindset.[7]

# break it down: gratitude

1. Start by listing all the people you are grateful for in your life, with your immediate support system first (parents, siblings, children, spouse, and so on). If you have lost people who belong in this first circle, be sure to include them even though they're gone.

2. Now expand that list out to the next level of people you care about, like your friends, and then the level beyond that, including everyone else who makes your daily routine better, like your coworkers (the nice ones) or the magazine-stand guy who always gives you a free pack of gum.

3. Acknowledge your gratitude for your health and the health of those you care for.

4. Next list all the opportunities, past and present, you are grateful you have had: going to a certain school (Go HC!), an old job, current clients, and so on.

5. Now inventory your current challenges or losses, or difficult people who are on your mind. Find just one positive thing you have taken away from each experience. This is the hardest part, and believe me, I've come up with some weird take-aways (an actual recent Nacie gratitude: "I am grateful this person taught me that sometimes being a b*tch is the only way to stand up for yourself"). Sometimes the only thing you can do is be grateful you had something, even though it's now gone ("I am grateful I had the chance to work with Jones & Jones, even though they dropped me for another vendor"). You might not really mean it at the time, but trust me, saying it out loud or to yourself can make a big impact, even sub-consciously, as you memorialize and let go of the experience.

6. I like to close my gratitude list by feeling thankful I have another day before me to do my best, try my hardest, and work toward my goals. I encourage you to close your list in what-ever way feels most fitting for you.

## Keep Hope Alive

A final key resilience tactic that future members of the Fittest will find valuable as they prepare to adopt the gig mindset is the ability to "maintain a hopeful outlook." I don't want to get all touchy-feely on you, but what they say is true: You get what you expect from life—or in this case your career. The APA explains that "an optimistic outlook enables you to expect that good things will happen in your life . . . rather than worrying about what you fear." Much of what we fear as modern professionals is out of our hands: we can't control how good our competition is or how rapidly the workforce globalizes; we can't stop the invention of new, job-reducing technologies. But that doesn't stop us from thinking about these things, fretting about them, and getting down on ourselves over them. One of the key strategies you can use to reduce such negative thoughts and cultivate a hopeful outlook is monitoring and promoting positive self-talk.[8]

Self-talk is exactly what it sounds like: it is how we talk to ourselves inside our own minds. Also referred to as our internal voice, self-talk can be an empowering or destructive force depending on what language or tone we allow it to take. A person's internal voice can play a number of different roles, from the chastising parent to the kid who wants something to the logical intellectual. Some people struggle with a borderline abusive internal voice, while others have one that rationalizes and justifies everything they do, right or wrong. Many of us are unaware of our self-talk, even though it is running constantly through our thoughts like the news crawl at the bottom of a television screen, and equally unaware of how it positively or negatively affects our perspective.

The big challenge of learning to monitor self-talk is in tuning into something that you have been tuning out, likely for years. Unfortunately, there is no great trick for it: you just need to start being mindful of how you internally respond to the various elements of your day. Once you successfully tune into that voice and observe it, you can begin to make adjustments to reduce negative commentary and enhance positive self-talk. In an article condensing the research on self-talk, the Mayo Clinic staff suggests an effective rule to use when improving the attitude of your self-talk: don't allow yourself to say anything internally that you wouldn't say to someone else. This will keep you from adding unnecessary stress to yourself through self-judgment or other limiting beliefs.[9]

Monitoring and adjusting self-talk can feel like a lot of work, especially if you are unfamiliar with the technique. But remember that your commitment can pay off in more ways than just upping your psychological resilience: studies have shown that maintaining a hopeful outlook can increase your lifespan and even improve your immune response to things like the common cold. With fringe benefits like that, it's no wonder that the Fittest are keeping their thoughts positive in spite of the economic chaos![10]

When you are feeling anxious about the future, it's sometimes difficult to stay positive. The result is that negative self-talk can start to creep into your thought process, perpetuating the anxiety and preventing your gig mindset from accessing the right perspective.

Keeping a positive attitude is key to being able to recognize opportunities in your environment. This is because when you are in a positive mood, your thinking is more expansive and possibility-oriented. To help keep your mood and thinking on track, try making "coping cards." When you notice negative self-talk, use the cards to remind yourself of positive thoughts that will help you think about possibilities. Here is an adaptation of a standard exercise that you can use regularly:

## break it down: coping cards

This is an adapted cognitive-behavioral therapy technique that can help you manage adversity and positively direct your self-talk.

Coping cards are business-size cards that contain positive statements such as:

"I have overcome adversity in the past and I can do it again."
"I am mentally strong and can live with this."
"I can tolerate this uncertainty and use it to my advantage."
"I am stronger than my problems."
"Good things are in store for me in the future."
"For every problem there is more than one solution."

Make out your coping cards when you are in a good mood. Then carry them with you, post them on your bathroom mirror, or keep them prominently displayed on your computer to anticipate and preempt negative self-talk.[11]

## asking the right questions

A week or so after Renee had shared the story of her career journey with me, I found myself staring at my notes, feeling like something was missing. The interview had lasted for several hours, and we had covered seemingly every nuance of her story, from college background to the hopelessness unemployment breeds. But there was still a piece of the story that didn't seem complete. I read my notes again for the twentieth time . . . and then it came to me. I grabbed my phone and placed the call.

"Hello?" I could hear her three miniature poodles yip-yipping excitedly in the background.

"Hi Renee, it's Nacie." I found myself yelling into the receiver to keep from being drowned out by the poodle choir. "I just needed to follow up on something from our interview."

"Yeah, sure, what's up?" She shushed the dogs, and the sound of a door shutting in the background let me know I had her full attention.

"You said that you *realized* you had to think about your post-PwC jobs as a way to build your skills, even though they didn't move you up your career ladder. How did you *realize* that?"

The line was silent for a minute, and I worried the connection had been lost. "Well," she said at last, exhaling loudly, "I guess I just started asking myself the right questions."

Aha.

Members of the Fittest begin to adopt the gig mindset by asking questions. Not just any questions, mind you, but as Renee put it, the *right* questions.

Asking questions may seem like an easy tactic—almost too easy—for tackling the huge mental shift involved in taking ownership of your career. But the *right questions* can be truly powerful things. They can act as catalysts that spark amazing transformations. And the ability to both ask yourself the right questions and elicit the corresponding answers is influenced by the strength of your ability to psychologically adapt. This is why building up your emotional resilience is a vital preparation to taking the leap and adopting the gig mindset.

Yet if there are right questions, then that presupposes there are *wrong* questions as well. I remember being in a lecture in college and feeling profoundly affected by the professor's argument that the most important question in human existence is: *Knowing we will die, how then shall we live?*[12]

I am sure this question is pretty standard fare for college lectures, but it really affected me. We all know we are going to die; that is a certainty. And the questions about when, where, and how are inconsequential because they are typically out of our control. These questions, the professor argued, are the wrong questions, because we can rarely take ownership for how we die. But we can take ownership for how we live, even with the ominous threat of death hovering somewhere ahead of us. So "How shall we live?" is a right question—maybe the great granddaddy of all right questions.

In a job market like today's, there are lots of questions you can ask yourself: *When are things getting better? Will I lose my job? What's going to happen to the unemployment rate? What's going to happen to me?*

These questions are wrong questions, because they have no answers that you or I or anyone else can give with reasonable certainty or authority. Like the details of your death, they are in many ways outside of your control. Sure, you could flip off a client and get fired, or push a wrong button in your investment software and cause another global crash that shoots the unemployment rate to 30 percent (kidding: personal investment software can't really do that . . . right?). But outside of such situations, you have no ownership in the answers to these questions, which is why they are wrong questions.

The wrong questions—and there are thousands you can pose about your career in this economy—have two defining characteristics:

- They place ownership of the answer with a higher power (for example, the economy, your organization, the gods)
- They do not elicit an actionable response

Think about the hypothetical question *Am I going to lose my job?* The asker is powerless to affect the answer—it is in a higher authority's control—and there is no clear call to action that results from the question. What can you do with a question like this? How can you respond with forward-moving action? Where can it really get you as you try to let go of your preconceived career notions and embrace and own a new career future?

The answer is nowhere. Those who get stuck in a cycle of asking themselves these questions are the very same people who find themselves waiting for things to go back to normal. After all, when you are asking yourself questions that you can't answer and that provoke no response on your end (or at least none that are grounded in fact), there isn't much left for you to do except wait for someone else to figure things out.

Now let's consider the right questions.

The right questions about your career, as you may guess, are the antitheses of the wrong questions. Additionally, they work to overcome the confirmation biases that keep you from driving your career. The three key characteristics of right questions are:

- They squarely place ownership, power, and control of your career ladder on your shoulders
- They naturally call you to some form of action

- They address and effectively challenge any confirmation bias and break preconceptions that cause waiting and inaction

But how can you challenge your confirmation bias effectively? Didn't we just learn that it takes considerably more effort to convince someone of something that goes against his or her preconceived beliefs?

Contrarian lines of questioning—questions that purposely call upon the responder to answer from the opposing point of view—are very effective in drawing individuals outside of their confirmation bias or other limiting psychological perspectives. By asking a professional like yourself to look at the future of your career ladder from a different perspective, I am requiring you to move beyond your bias barriers and see possibilities outside of your usual conceptions. This is exactly what we want to do to when forging our future.

So what would a right question look like? Right questions are any combination of the three criteria mentioned above: they challenge career confirmation bias; they place ownership on you; and they promote actionable responses. Several key phrases can be used to set a contrarian tone when formulating a right question. They include:

- "For the sake of argument . . . "
- "Let's play devil's advocate and pretend . . . "
- "Just imagine that . . . "
- "Let's assume . . . "
- "What if . . . "

Clearly these phrases alone won't do much. However, when paired with an actionable question or phrase that shifts ownership onto you, they become powerful tools for establishing your gig mindset and opening you up to the real opportunities of a new job market.

Here are some great examples:

- For the sake of argument, let's say the job market is never going back to how it was prerecession: is my original career path realistic?
- Let's assume I won't be able to find employment in my field over the next six months: what other fields of employment can I pursue?
- What if I never make partner thanks to the company tightening its belt? What else could I work toward that would make my career a success by *my* standards?

You can even reframe any wrong question to a right question simply by using a combination of the three right question criteria. For example:

| Wrong Question | Reframed Right Question |
|---|---|
| "When are things getting better?" | "I can't know when or how things will get better. What can I do this week to make my résumé stronger?" |
| "Will I lose my job?" | "For argument's sake, let's say I lose my job. How can I present my skills in the most dynamic way to other employers?" |
| "What's going to happen to the unemployment rate?" | "Let's assume unemployment is going to rise. How can I make myself even more indispensable to my employer?" |
| "What's going to happen to me?" | "I can't predict what will happen to me, but I do know that whatever happens, I'll do better the more adaptable I am. What can I learn this year that will round out my skill set and make me more adaptable?" |

Just like the difference between the Fittest and everyone else, the difference between a wrong question and a right question is really about perspective. Now that's a comforting thought.

It's all well and good to read about the right questions, but it is another thing entirely to sit down and ask (and answer) them for yourself. Below I have compiled a list of questions that members of the Fittest reported using effectively in some form (a number of them have appeared as examples in this chapter). Working with these questions put the power of their careers in their hands and snapped them out of waiting for things to go back to normal. I encourage you to craft your own set of right questions tailored to your specific situation and industry.

## break it down: the right questions

I want you to read through the following questions a few times and then mull them over. Think about them in the car; think about them in the shower; think about them whenever you have a spare moment to yourself. Your instinct may be to answer them right away, but letting go of something—whether it is an expectation for your career or your love of boy bands—involves taking time to process and understand. After you have given the questions some thought, I want you to answer the ones that resonate with you and your position. I hope you'll consider writing down these answers, or sharing them with friends, to enhance the power of their punch.

- For the sake of argument, let's say the job market is never going back to how it was prerecession: are my original career and the associated goals realistic?
- Let's assume I won't be able to find employment in my field over the next six months: what other fields of employment can I pursue?

- Let's assume my career ladder is stalled: how can I use this time to my advantage?
- What certification would I need to complete to increase my earning power in this economic climate?
- What if I don't find a job in my degree field of study: how can I frame and apply my skill set to another industry?
- Let's imagine I've gone as far as I can in this particular organization: what can I do to make myself attractive to other organizations within my field?
- What skills do I need to master to do my type of work most effectively?
- What can I do this week to make my résumé stronger?
- For argument's sake, let's say I lose my job: how can I present my skills in the most dynamic way to other employers?
- Let's assume unemployment is going to rise: what skills can I improve to make myself even more indispensable to my present employer and attractive to others?
- What can I learn this year that will round out my skill set and make me more adaptable?
- For the sake of argument, let's say that I am unfulfilled in this industry: is it time for me to consider shifting gears to a new field or career track?

When you ask yourself the right questions about your career, you want to be especially sure your self-talk voice is switched into neutral gear. As you reflect on these questions, try to leave judgment ("I should have worked harder"), nagging "what-ifs" ("I should have worked in a different field"), and over-rationalizations of your choices thus far ("Don't worry, you did everything fine") out of your responses. These questions are meant to objectively challenge beliefs and perceptions, and so the tone in which you pose them to yourself and respond should reflect that.

The funny thing about us humans is that not having the power or authority to control something has never kept us from thinking that if we worry about it long enough or hard enough somehow we can influence the outcome. Yet at the end of the day, myriad factors at play are outside of our control, affecting daily life. And we are in a position to control just about none of them (if you have developed a weather-making machine, then you need to share it with me ASAP!).

If you find yourself having a difficult time reflecting on these questions, try using this simple method to mentally move forward: find an empty box or drawer somewhere in your home and dub it the "Above My Pay Grade" space. When you find yourself occupied by thoughts that fall into the category of "uncontrollable" or "unanswerable," write them down on an index card and put them in your "Above My Pay Grade" space—then give yourself permission to let them go. After all, you've actually done something now: you've brought the question or concern to the attention of something bigger and more in the loop than you, be it God, the Universe, or the company CEO you're not at liberty to communicate with. You can now get back to the business of your business: thriving.

## sliding into the driver's seat

By adjusting your perspective and harnessing the power of your resilience, you are allowing your career to be so much more than just a journey from one employer to another. You are owning it and guiding it as it evolves into a unique entity.

Before we move on to the rest of the strategies, I want you to ask yourself just one more question:

*Am I ready and willing to take ownership of my career and place its power in my hands?*

It may seem like a silly question—even moot at this point—but you have to ask. As Peter Parker's uncle says, "With great power comes great responsibility."

By utilizing the first strategy of the Finch Effect, you are opening yourself up to all the potential and opportunity that ownership provides. You realize that your career success is in your hands, whether you are working within an employer-based model or for yourself. You understand that no job market, be it a good one or a bad one, is going to define who you are as a professional or keep you from moving forward.

However, you are also opening yourself up to all the responsibility that comes with ownership. This includes responsibility for figuring out what happened and what to do when things go wrong—because things do go wrong, and it can feel quite painful when they do so on your watch. Someone could tell you that once you make the switch to the gig mindset it will be all smooth sailing and that you'll never stress about work again and everything will go your way. But I can't tell you that, and wouldn't want to even if I could. What I can tell you from my own experience thus far is that the most interesting career journeys have hills and valleys; they aren't walks across flat land or straight shots up a career ladder.

By building up your psychological resilience and asking the right questions of yourself and your career, you are letting go of waiting for someone else to dictate what happens to your career, and you are also taking on the responsibility of figuring out that next move for yourself. This ownership is the very heart of adaptation. The finches couldn't wait around for food sources to adapt to them, just as Renee couldn't sit in a dead-end job and wait for an opportunity to present itself to her. She had to challenge her preconceived notions of her career and use questions—the right ones—as a tool to claim control and decide her next move.

You can't waste one more day of your life wondering if the stars are going to align to move your career forward, give you a job, or reveal a premade career path. You are a fledging member of the Fittest, and the Fittest forge their own future.

So I ask you again: Are you ready and willing to take ownership of your career and place its power in your hands?

Thought so.

Now let's get down to the task of helping you stand out from the vocational crowd. Let's identify your professional value.

# 3

# identify your
# professional value

Depending on the season, there can be as many as fifty-eight distinct species of birds inhabiting the Galápagos Islands. Twenty-eight of those species live on the islands year-round, and thirteen of *those* species are finches. This means that depending on the time of year, finches account for roughly one quarter to one half of the avian species on the islands. During his voyage on the *Beagle*, Darwin puzzled over how so many different types of finches could not only survive together but thrive together on the island chain. What was the conclusion he arrived at decades later? Variation and differentiation.

As a modern professional, you might recognize these two concepts not as keys for surviving the volcanic landscape of the Galápagos but as effective business practices. In corporate jargon, they are better recognized by the terms *value proposition* and *competitive differentiation*. According to Anthony

K. Tjan, a venture capitalist and blogger for the *Harvard Business Review*, an organization's *value proposition* is the sum total of the responses to three key questions:

1. What product or service is the company selling?
2. Who is the target customer?
3. What makes the company's offering unique or different?

Once this value proposition is defined, it gets translated into the organization's *competitive differentiation* by the sales and marketing departments. If you are unfamiliar with this term, you can think of it as the effective branding and messaging of the value proposition. The goal of competitive differentiation is to have the most compelling value proposition that is communicated in the most persuasive way to your target audience so that you are differentiated from the competition in a way that gives you the advantage.[1]

In the *Origin of Species*, Darwin wrote that "the preservation of individual differences and variations" is at the heart of understanding how survival of the fittest works. Differentiation and variation are the very crux of adaptability: they are the means of making a place for yourself within the context of an ever-shifting environment and also among other individuals within the environment. Variation and differentiation are adaptive (as Darwin noted) as long as those distinctions are "beneficial to the being under its conditions of life."[2] That is, variation that supports the goals and needs of the individual marks a member of the Fittest in any ecosystem—including the economic one.

The Galápagos finches can teach us a thing or two about variation. Across the thirteen species are some that live in trees and some that live on the ground. Depending on the species, a bird may eat fruit, insects, seeds, or even cactuses, and each species has a unique beak shape adapted to one or more functions: probing, crushing, grasping. These various traits—and myriad others—combine in a host of ways to create thirteen unique and distinguishable species of birds that can live together in a small area without stepping on each other's toes . . . or whatever kind of foot things finches have.

In the previous chapter, we explored how adopting the gig mindset can help you take ownership of your career and control of your professional survival. In this chapter, we will focus on how purposeful variation and differentiation can help you stand out from the crowd and fuel your vocational success. This is the core of the Finch Effect's second strategy: *Identify your professional value.*

We certainly aren't going to spend the next pages determining what shape your beak should be or whether you should eat insects or cactuses, although I hear both are yummy choices. But we are going to spend this time working on the professional human equivalent: your adaptive professional brand.

Over the last several years, I have observed members of the Fittest using what I call an *adaptive professional brand* (APB) to help leverage and package their professional value. The APB can encompass anything and everything from physical presentation, to skills and education, to an individual mission statement. Just like the corporate concepts of value proposition and competitive differentiation, successful APBs are designed to effectively communicate a compelling presentation of your professional services and unique value to your target market. APBs call upon you to utilize your gig mindset and channel your inner Jay-Z: "I'm not a businessman, I'm a *business,* man."

You can think of your target market as the customers you are trying to sell your brand to. For most professionals, the target markets are typically their current employer, a future employer, or a client. For example, if you currently work at a company that you would like to remain affiliated with or get promoted in, your target market for your APB is your current employer. Within that market, the customers for your brand may be one person who holds the keys to your advancement, or a group of people whom you need to affiliate with or impress to achieve your professional goals. For this customer, the main value you need to communicate through your APB is how you already meet and exceed the needs of the organization and how you are eager to grow in value to benefit the organization.

If you are unemployed, underemployed, or a soon-to-be college graduate, then you will likely choose the "future employer" option as your target market. Customers in this market can be hiring managers, human resource professionals, recruiters, or even people at networking events. When projecting your brand to these customers, you should be highlighting the value you have the potential to bring to their organization.

If you are an entrepreneur, freelancer, small business owner, or in an entrepreneurial industry (insurance brokerage, law, medical practice), then you will tailor your APB to the third market option, "clients" (or "patients"). When selling your brand to these customers, you would be wise to emphasize how your services or products have helped other clients with similar needs.

The reason I call these professional brands "adaptive" is that like all things in the Finch Effect universe, they are capable of evolving and growing with you and your career, especially in the context of your target market. You will likely not be job hunting, lobbying for advancement in a company, or selling to the same clients for your entire career, so it is important that you build a brand that can journey with you as the job environment changes and as you change as a professional.

Whenever I mention the concept of professional branding, the first things people think of are the *corporate brands* that saturate our daily lives (think Apple, Pepsi, Staples), or the *personal brands* that saturate our daily communication channels (think Kim Kardashian, Taylor Swift, Barack Obama). The problem with being surrounded by all this larger-than-life branding is that we forget what these brands, at their most foundational level, are created to do: they are for making products, services, and individuals stand out from the competition. My trusty American Heritage dictionary has reminded me that the formal definition of a brand does not include anything about multimillion dollar ad campaigns or reality television shows. A brand can be simply defined as a "distinctive category; a particular kind" of anything. In the context of this definition, we could even go so far as to say that each of the thirteen species of finch is its own "brand" of bird.

Professional brands—adaptive or otherwise—sit somewhere in the middle of the spectrum between a corporate brand and a personal brand. Like their corporate counterparts, professional brands communicate to the world what "product" is being offered to the target market or consumer, whether that product is a service, skill set, body of experience, or actual physical product. However, like their personal cousins, professional brands can also communicate to the world some key intangibles about an individual, such as the person's values, personality, and overall mission. One of the most common questions about professional brands is how they differ from personal brands. Alison Doyle, a human resource expert and

guide for About.com's Job Searching page, explained it best:
"Your professional brand is what [about you] matters to a potential employer, networking contact, or anyone who can help
you find a job or grow your career."[3]

When it comes to thriving in today's economy, Susan
Walaszek, the founder of HR Compliance Consulting, notes
that projecting a well-defined professional brand has a "significant impact on employers." In fact, the projection and leveraging of a professional brand can help your target market
determine "not only if you can perform the job but whether
you will fit in with the culture of the company."[4]

However, most American workers aren't accustomed to
seeing themselves as a brand. Or even worse, they mistake the
organization they work for as their brand. While I was
researching for this book, I asked Emily—a smart, educated,
and driven twenty-something—about her professional brand.
Her response shocked me a bit: "I haven't ever thought of myself as a brand. Instinctively, I guess I've always associated my
'brand' with the organization I am working for."

What I found as I continued to interview people on this
topic is that Emily's perception is not the exception but the
norm. And when you think about it, can you be surprised? If
you work forty hours a week, that means you are clocking in
around two thousand hours at your job per year, assuming you
get a two-week vacation. If you work at that rate from age 21 to
65, that can mean you spend almost ninety thousand hours of
your life at your job. Those numbers don't make the point for
you? Then let's consider it this way: if you rise at 7 A.M. and go
to bed around 11 P.M. and work from 9 A.M. to 5 P.M., that means
that of the sixteen hours you are awake during the day, eight of
them—or one half—are spent at your place of work. That

doesn't include commute time or the less quantifiable "I am thinking about something for work right now even though I am at my kid's soccer game" time.

Our jobs, whether they are part of a larger career plan or just something to make a little green with, are huge parts of our daily lives. They aren't something separate that exists in little vacuums of time. It is no wonder then that the individuals I connected with mentioned the companies they worked for as major elements of their professional brand. It was only members of the Fittest who thought otherwise.

Perceiving the organization you work for to be an elemental part of your professional brand is not only an antiquated notion reminiscent of William H. Whyte's definition of an "Organization Man," but also a serious liability in an age when organizations shed workers as easily as a cocker spaniel sheds fur. Individuals who perceive their company as their brand are setting themselves up for a major professional identity crisis if they ever part ways with the organization, even voluntarily. And I think we can all agree, knowing what we know about the forces shaping the job market, that anyone's staying at just one organization for an entire career is highly improbable.[5]

In the rest of this chapter, we will dive deeply into the concept of adaptive professional branding, outline the APB components that members of the Fittest have found vital for their success, and begin to identify and craft your own APB. Finally, we will put it all together to help you identify how you can best leverage this brand for your own success. By the end of this chapter, you will have a clear sense of what your professional value proposition is and how to communicate it effectively to your target market.

Let's build a brand.

## the value of crafting an apb

I've had people ask me if defining a professional brand is the best use of their time in this tough economy: "Shouldn't I be spending my time sending out résumés or something?" But here's the thing: you already have a professional brand. Everything about you is constantly coming together and being communicated to the outside world. Everyone already sees a "You, Inc.," especially in the workplace. As Susan Walaszek points out, "The résumé and interview presentation, the clothing one wears, the events one attends, and the body language of the individual all are a type of branding in terms of the level of professionalism, approachability, and personality."[6]

But if you don't consciously refine and project a particular brand, then what "You, Inc." is communicating to the world on your behalf is up to the gods. In the best-case scenario, you aren't actively leveraging your assets and are missing opportunities; in the worst-case scenario, you are projecting a message that is inaccurate, unhelpful, or damaging.

We often fail to realize that while every single person is a complex and multifaceted individual, we are perceived by most of the world through a small set of relatively simple and one-dimensional terms. John is driven and funny. Suzy is quiet and thorough. Brad is clownish and irresponsible. Don't believe me? Think about someone you work with whom you don't know very well. Do you have a robust conception of their life experience, skill sets, passions, goals, and preferences, or do you have a couple of adjectives on mental file? Yeah, that's what I thought.

Of course, the longer and more intimately you know someone, the more your perception of them expands outside of basic descriptors. Yet in a business world where many career-altering decisions can be made quickly and on the basis of just a few interactions, it behooves us to actively communicate an easily digestible professional brand that projects the right descriptors to our target market.

There are other major benefits to be gained from taking the time to outline your adaptive professional brand. One of these is an increase in your professional worth. The clearer and more confident you can be about your value and differentiation from the competition, the more you are worth to employers or clients. Professional worth translates as tangible worth (compensation and benefits) and intangible worth (value to an organization, reputation), and in this economy both are essential. When you know what you bring to the table and can firmly assert it, you can command more for your talent.

Communicating an adaptive professional brand can also improve your networking success. The ability to communicate your brand concisely to others improves your capacity to network. Not only will it help you project a consistent message about who you are as a professional and support your reputation; it will also help you engage better with others. Instead of fumbling around for an answer to "So, tell me, what you do?" you have a succinct response on hand so that you can spend the conversation learning about the other person and making valuable connections.

One of the most underrecognized but important benefits of building and maintaining an APB is that it gives you a guide for skill development. Should you get that MBA? Is executive coaching a good use of your resources? An awareness of your differentiated value can help you pursue investments of your time and capital that continue to strengthen your value proposition and help you weed out random focuses that don't tie into your larger brand. We will talk more about skill development in the context of your APB in the next chapter.

Finally, your adaptive professional brand can be your vocational North Star. Brands are not just projections of what other people can expect from you; they can also serve as reminders of what you can expect from yourself and where you want to go. In a world full of distractions, flash-in-the-pan pundits, and shiny objects, a clear sense of what you bring to the table as a unique professional can help you maintain your sense of career ownership and identity through good economic times and bad. It can also provide you a foundation for coherent adaptation, growth, and expansion of your skill set over the course of your career. I can tell you from my own career journey that I identified writing as part of my APB long before I had a column or book contract. Building that into my brand helped me achieve that goal by keeping me focused on seeking out opportunities for development that supported it.

These are the most common and powerful ways adaptive professional brands can provide value for you on your vocational journey, yet they aren't the only ones. Beyond career benefits, the process of building and maintaining an APB can be a real quest for self-discovery, self-understanding, and self-acceptance. I encourage you to embrace it and engage with it fully and go where it takes you, whether to a different perspective on your job or to a totally new career. Remember what I said in Chapter One: the unexpected opportunity in all this job market change is a freedom to forge a new way forward.

Of course, to enjoy all these benefits you'll need to start building your adaptive professional brand. Let's start by reviewing the key components.

# break it down: your personal strengths

Your adaptive professional brand focuses on what strengths you posses as a worker. However, taking an opportunity to also define your personal strengths can indirectly help your brand by bolstering your confidence and helping you build a brand as a professional that is in line with who you are as a person. By knowing your strengths, you can choose responsibilities at work and at home that are in tune with your strong points.

To begin to define your strengths, write out a list of every strength you have as a whole person. This can include strengths you have as a professional, a parent, a child, a friend, or a hobby enthusiast. If you're having trouble getting started, check out this list of example strengths for inspiration:

- optimistic
- responsible
- honest
- intelligent
- competent
- precise
- imaginative
- loving
- persevering
- organized
- enthusiastic
- inventive
- adventurous

Another way to approach building your strengths list is to think about an important moment or decision in your life (or more than one) and consider what strengths you exhibited in that story. What do your choices, behavior, or strategy in that instance say about your strengths and gifts? You can also feel free to ask your close friends, family, and even your coworkers what they see as your strengths to help round out your list.

Once your list is complete, reflect on each trait and think back to a recent time when it was on display. After you have acknowledged each trait, rank them in order, giving the most prominent strength you have identified the number 1. Pick the five top strengths and write them on an index card preceded by the words "I am . . . " These are your core personal strengths.

## the components of an apb

There are some things that every finch has: beak, feathers, eyes, those foot things. These elements are not what make one species of finch different from another; in fact, they are what unify them as birds (rather than mammals, fish, or any other kind of animal).

What distinguishes one species of finch from the others are the specific characteristics of these common elements—how big the beak is, what color the feathers are, how close together the eyes are—and how they combine in the individuals of a species.

You can think of your adaptive professional brand in the same way: a set of basic components are common to all effective APBs. In fact, an APB wouldn't really be an APB without them. But the specific details and combinations of these components make each brand unique and differentiated.

The components of an effective APB serve two primary goals:

1. To help you outline your value as an individual professional
2. To help you stand out from the competition

The major components that support these two goals can be broken into three categories: presentation, offering, and mission. After we explore each of these categories in detail, we will use them to outline your own APB.

### Presentation

The presentation category addresses all visual representations of your brand, and can be broken down into three subcategories: physical presentation, paper presentation, and digital presentation. Physical presentation has to do with things like hairstyle, fashion choices, makeup, hygiene, piercings, tattoos, and even how you tie your tie. Additionally, it includes things like physical poise, eye contact, and overall projection of presence.

I refer to the second presentation subcategory as "paper presentation" because it encompasses the items we mean when we say, "Well, he looks good on paper"—even though admittedly much of what falls in this arena is now digitized. Paper presentation includes not only the visual appearance (design) but also the accuracy, structure, grammatical correctness, and eloquence of your résumé, cover letters, e-mails, snail-mail letters, and even text messages. Depending on your industry, articles, summaries, briefs, reports, or other written documentation can also fall into this subcategory. The fonts used, letterhead, citation format, and tone of the writing can all influence how paper presentation works in the context of your APB.

The final presentation subcategory is digital presentation. As just noted, many of the items that fall into the paper presentation subcategory could now technically be labeled as digital presentation. So let's be clear that this subcategory really refers to your online presence (social media, website, and online pictures and videos). In our technological age, this subcategory of presentation is more important than ever for your APB, which is why we will be spending an entire chapter diving deeper into this part of your brand.

## Offering

Within an adaptive professional brand the offering category refers to what many consider to be the heart and soul of an individual's value proposition: his or her skills, talents, and experience. This category includes the broad strokes—the companies you have worked for, the titles you have held, the degrees you have earned—as well as the particulars, like experience with particular clients, specific job tasks performed, and courses you completed for your degrees. The offering portion of an APB is the concrete proof of what you bring to the table as a professional and speaks to what matters most to your target market: performance and results.

## Mission

The mission category of an APB is the most nebulous element but often the most powerful. It represents the grander, overarching goals and vision of your career. It is often referred to as a personal mission statement and can be explained as *why* you do what you do.

The reason the mission component is so integral to the APB is that, as business author Simon Sinek notes, "People don't buy *what* you do, they buy *why* you do it." His theory, called "The Golden Circle," suggests that most individuals and businesses spend too much time telling their target market what they do and how they do it, throwing the why in afterwards. But Sinek observes that most successful leaders and corporations gain loyal followings by explaining why they are motivated and driven to do their work, and then explaining what they do and how they do it as a support for why.[7]

When it comes to your adaptive professional brand, your target market likely won't be driven into enthusiastic fits over what you have done or how you have done it. It is the "why" factor that pulls it all together and makes the most powerful statement of your value proposition.

## Other Elements

There is a host of other elements that some people choose to include in their adaptive professional brand, like religious affiliation, educational affiliation, and professional association affiliation. I've had a few people consider including their hobbies and passions as components of the APB, or information about their family or upbringing. But unless that hobby or family story is specifically relevant to your field or can be understood in the context of a valuable professional experience or skill, I think such details can be irrelevant, distracting, or just unprofessional.

Each effective APB is a distinct recipe made up of these major categories of components. The secret to your "winning flavor" is how much of each component you draw from and what you put in those components. There is no specific formula for the perfect APB; it is something that is consciously crafted with each individual in mind.

## break it down: outlining your apb

You can start to outline what components your APB will include by answering the following questions. I recommend you go through and answer all the questions, and then go back and review and elaborate on your initial responses.

- Who did you identify as your target market? Why?
- What two or three descriptive terms would you ideally like to be associated with your professional brand?
- What do you consider the biggest selling point for your professional value proposition?
- Please force-rank the following APB categories in order of their importance for your brand: presentation, offering, mission.
- How would you describe your physical presentation in professional situations?

- What message do you want your résumé and cover letter to communicate to your target market?
- If someone only knew you through your e-mails, letters, or other writings, how would you want them to describe you?
- Do you currently have social media accounts set up (Facebook, Twitter, LinkedIn) and/or a personal website?
- What do you consider your top one to three professional skills?
- How would you describe your professional experience in two sentences or less?
- Can you identify an example of when your skills or experience specifically benefited a member of your target market?
- Do you have a vision for where you want to be in your career in the next five years? Ten years? Twenty years? If not, please take a few minutes to think about these and then respond.
- Why is this vision important to you?
- Why are you working in your current industry?
- What do you think makes you different from other professionals in your industry?
- Do you think your brand today represents how you want your brand to be perceived in the future?

As you review your answers to these questions, I want you to ask yourself if you feel this is the right set of pieces for your APB, of if something is missing. When you consider your answers as a whole, do you feel proud of or excited by the brand of your career, or does it just feel "blah"?

Your brand is what you are going to get up every day to advance, support, and promote. If it's not something you can totally get behind and support, then something has to change. If you are feeling "blah" about the sum of these parts, I encourage you to go back over and look at the responses to ask yourself what is not resonating with you. Maybe it's your physical presentation; maybe it's the clients you are working with; or maybe it's your industry. Whatever it is, just remember that you have the power to change anything. This is an *adaptive* professional brand, and if your career needs to be jazzed up or shift in another direction, then no worries—the work on your brand thus far can help support you in that transition.

Another possibility is that you might feel really energized by your APB but everyone else sees it as "blah." One of our biggest challenges as humans is seeing beyond our own perspective to understand how things appear to others. Often what we think is great, appropriate, or correct is perceived by others to be the exact opposite. Let's be honest, we've all worn that shirt or got that haircut that we thought looked fantastic, only to receive bewildered stares or smirks from people on the street. But questionable fashion sense aside, navigating the gap between how we see ourselves and how others perceive us is never more crucial than when we are building our professional brand. Just like a corporation, we can't just roll out a product because we think it is good; we need to do market research to understand if our vision is translating appropriately to the consumer.

## break it down: workshopping your apb

As a litmus test for how your draft APB is coming across, I recommend you ask one or two people to answer the following questions. Feel free to have family, friends, coworkers, or clients respond, as long as they have observed you in a professional capacity.

- What two or three descriptive terms do you associate with [your name]'s professional brand?
- What do you consider their biggest selling point for their professional value?
- How would you describe their physical presentation in professional situations?
- What messages do their written communications or reports project?
- What does their social media presence contribute to their professional success?
- What do you consider their top one to three professional skills to be?
- How would you describe their professional experience in two sentences or less?
- Can you identify an example of when their skills or experience specifically benefited their target market?
- Do you think they have a vision for where they want to be in their career in the next five years? Ten years? Twenty years?
- What motivates them to pursue their current line of work?
- Do they stand out from others in their industry? Why or why not?

When you receive the responses back, I want you to consider where your answers and their answers do or do not match up. For the items that match up, congratulations: you are projecting that component consistently. The responses that don't match up indicate that either you aren't communicating your message correctly or how you want to be seen isn't where you are yet. The best way to figure out whether it is the former or the latter is to have a dialogue with your responders about their answers. Show them your response and then ask them to help you figure out where the breakdown is. If it is the former, there are likely ways you can tweak something to correct the communication, like not wearing your Mohawk to work, not misspelling the boss's name, or remembering to mention your experience at Habitat for Humanity.

If it's the latter, then no worries: the next chapter is all about ramping up your skills to back up the content of your APB. But first, we have to put it all together.

## putting the pieces together

Your responses to the questions given earlier in the chapter (along with the responses you received from others) can be seen as the building blocks of your adaptive professional brand. They are the components that will be arranged together in a way that shares with the world your professional value proposition and differentiation. But figuring out how to put them together can feel a little puzzling . . . that is, if you don't know the three keys of professional branding.

The three keys are a set of deceptively simple questions that can help you laser-focus all the components you just outlined into a coherent package, one that can be leveraged and promoted to advance your career in any economy.

### Your Tagline

The first key asks, "What is your tagline?"

The tagline, also referred to as a brand slogan, is an amazing marketing tool that allows the value proposition of a product to be communicated in one short phrase. You have likely read or heard hundreds of taglines in your life, like Sprite's "obey your thirst," Nike's "just do it," or—my personal favorite—"the truth is out there" from *The X-Files* (love you, Mulder!). Like these examples prove, when you get them right, taglines are memorable, easily identifiable, and inextricably attached to the product in the minds of the target market.

## four ways to build the credibility of your apb

1. **Create a website.** The first and most important thing you can do for yourself to establish credibility online is create a professional website that outlines your APB. I recommend a blog format that includes a résumé section and an "about me" section. A good way to organize your site is to model it after another professional site you find visually appealing.

2. **Join an industry-relevant network.** There are hosts of professional organizations around the country that focus on connecting professionals in every job function imaginable. Do a Google search with some keywords and your city name to find out where and when your peers are connecting.

3. **Participate in blog discussions.** Another person's blog is an excellent place for you to gain exposure. To find blogs on topics in your field or industry, simply follow the search suggestion above using the word "blog" instead of "network."

4. **Attend industry-relevant fairs, shows, and exhibitions.** Professionals go to conferences and industry fairs to observe the latest in their craft but also to meet their peers and competition and make professional contacts of all kinds. If you are feeling confident in your skill level, think about participating in one of these gatherings. Bring your business cards and a pad and pen to jot down any tips or tricks you hear, any names and numbers that aren't printed on the cards you collect, and general impressions about what you see and whom you meet.

For members of the Fittest, a tagline that captures the essence of their APB can be an effective way to communicate their brand through specific channels like business cards or social media profiles (which we'll discuss more in Chapter Five). Several styles of taglines can be employed, depending on what you are working to communicate with your overall brand. I'll list them below with actual examples of taglines from the Fittest (if you can guess which one is mine, you'll get a prize—just kidding):

- The mission-focused tagline (example: *On a quest to make my passion for blogging my business*)
- The role-focused tagline (example: *Professional development author and career evolutionist*)
- The personality-focused tagline (example: *Crafty, Creative, and Ready to Go!*)
- The value-focused tagline (example: *The number one artisan bread in the state*)

Coming up with your tagline is arguably the most fun part of developing your APB because you get to play big-firm copywriter for a few minutes. But building your tagline is also enjoyable because to a big extent you are crafting it for your personal benefit and private use.

More than any other part of your APB, your tagline can be used as an easily accessible touchstone to remind yourself who you are, what you want, and what you are doing as a professional. Sure, it will be used in various places online and in print. But it won't be spoken aloud or used to introduce yourself to others in person (imagine the Nike CEO using his company's tagline to explain his value proposition at a cocktail party—doesn't work). So aside from its print uses, the tagline is yours to add to your personal crawl line of positive self-talk.

However, this self-serving aspect of your tagline should not encourage you to settle on a tagline you think is mysterious or cool; to everyone else, it may seem cryptic or nonsensical. For example, tagging yourself as "The One" might seem like a witty nod to *The Matrix* and a reflection of your superiority among your industry peers. But to everyone who doesn't know you (that is, your target market), it likely translates as an incomplete or presumptuous assertion. "The one" what? And why?

As the old marketing adage goes, it is always better to be clear, not clever. Here are some other parameters for developing your tagline:

- Try to keep your tagline under fifteen words for easy memorization and recognition
- Craft it with your target market in mind
- Keep it consistent with the core elements of your brand
- If you are going to be sassy or cute, don't overdo it—be consistent with the other parameters in this list
- Make sure any role-focused taglines reflect your gig mindset, not your organizational title (example: "Social Media Strategist" instead of "Director of Social Media for Jones Insurance")
- Be descriptive about your experience, offering, or services
- Project confidence, capability, and professionalism appropriate to your industry and career level
- Resist outrageous claims, clichés, or cheesy language ("You've tried the rest, now try the best!")
- Strive for compelling, but when in doubt, keep it conservative

Crafting an effective tagline not only allows you to communicate your APB quickly and effectively to others but also provides a way to easily reinforce your core message to yourself. That can come in handy when someone asks you to respond to the second key question of APB marketing: your story.

## Your Story: Short Version

"What is your story?" The opportunity to present your APB won't always be prompted with this exact phrase. Other questions that ask for the same response include "So, tell me about yourself" and "So, what do you do?" Earlier we talked about how we are perceived by most of the world as just a few choice descriptors: smart and successful, lazy and irresponsible, cute and friendly. People define us in these terms not necessarily out of indifference to our complexity as individuals but because it is in our brain physiology to filter and categorize those around us—think of it as a vestigial survival mechanism or a kissing cousin to confirmation bias. In an interview on 20/20, John Dovidio, a psychology professor from the University of Connecticut, noted, "When you are a social animal, you need to be able to distinguish who's a friend and who's a foe. You need to understand who's a member of your pack, who's a member of a different pack. . . . We categorize people automatically, unconsciously, immediately."[8]

Yet we all know from our own experience that the one thing that suddenly brings depth and dimension to an individual we've categorized and filed away with descriptors is hearing that person's story. The guy who lives down the hall from you is just noisy and unfriendly in your mind, until you hear the story about how his wife left him for his brother and hasn't let him see his daughter in years.

Suddenly, that man no longer fits neatly into that descriptor box; he is a human being that you are more aware of and sympathetic to.

While members of the Fittest don't go around telling every employer, job prospect, or client their entire life story, they do recognize the value of sharing their professional story as a way to stand out from their competition. By themselves the components of your APB are just pieces of information; someone might use them to refine the descriptors they give you. But on their own, they won't make you stand out. It is how you weave the pieces into your story—the story of your adaptive professional brand— that brings them to life and out of that descriptor box.

This is why I feel it is so valuable to make the third component category—the mission—a foundational element of your brand. If you are struggling to understand what your professional brand is all about, I recommend you frame it a little differently in your mind as "What is my professional mission, and how do my offering, presentation, and goals support that mission?"

You should have two distinct versions of your story on tap: a two-minute version and a fifteen-minute version. The two-minute version is the "elevator speech" of your APB. The elevator speech, so named because it is supposed to last no longer than an elevator ride, is a way for you to introduce the highlights of your value proposition to someone in your target market—be it your boss's boss, a potential employer, or a prospect—in a short, impressive blurb. This version is meant to whet the appetite of the person you are speaking with so they want to learn more about you. It is not a rambling monologue about all your qualifications or special skills but instead a few sentences, presented in a conversational style, that touch on the highlights of your APB and the value they provide to your target market.

When it comes to preparing the two-minute version of your story, I recommend sitting down and actually writing out a draft or two so you can wordsmith it to hit all the highlights of your APB. The average person can hear words most comfortably at a rate of about 150 to 160 words per minute, so your draft elevator speech should be about 300 words total, or two midsized paragraphs.[9]

When you draft your two-minute story, keep these guidelines in mind (you'll note similarities to the guidelines for writing your tagline):

- Develop the story with your target market in mind
- Make sure it is consistent with the core elements of your brand (presentation, offering, mission) as well as your tagline
- Don't rely too much on sass or cuteness—you don't want to sound like an amateur
- Be descriptive about your experience, offering, or services
- Project confidence, capability, and professionalism appropriate to your industry and career level
- Resist outrageous claims or cheesy language
- Strive for compelling, but when in doubt, keep it conservative

In addition, be sure you are using accessible language that works with appropriate vocal inflections and hand gestures; the language you choose should allow you to put yourself across naturally and dynamically. Remember, the point of the two-minute story is to share as much about your APB as possible and leave the target market wanting to learn more. Here is a good example of an elevator pitch from a member of the Fittest:

*I use my training in psychology to consult with and coach corporations and entrepreneurs in the Northeast about how to use creativity strategies to improve their problem-solving and team cohesion skills. Over the last few years, I've spent the majority of my time working with several government taskforces on developing creativity-based resilience training for homeless vets. This project is really close to my heart, because the reason I was drawn to this field of work was watching my uncle, a Vietnam vet, suffer with reintegrating into society after his tour of duty. You know, I remember being ten years old and wishing so badly that I could help him in some way—that's why it was such a dream come true for me when I was accepted into Princeton's psychology PhD program after completing my BA and Master's at Boston University.*

*After I finished my doctorate, I had an amazing opportunity to spend two years researching creativity and resilience in London with my dissertation advisor. While over there, I met my husband who was at the time the CEO of a boutique accounting firm, and it was through getting to know his staff that I realized how applicable creativity strategies are to effectiveness in business. When we got back to the States, I immediately started reaching out to my friends in the business community about their teams' needs around problem-solving and cohesion and began to develop a coaching program that was built based on common themes and needs that emerged across the 16 initial companies I surveyed. Ten years later, I've had a chance to work with over 100 companies across 8 major industries and can tell you that problem-solving is problem-solving, whether you are welding steel or trading on Wall Street. I just find it so fascinating that while modern technology has offered new ways to approach these key business issues, the methods at their core remain the same.*

What's good about this elevator speech is that it speaks about what the individual is offering (coaching and consulting services), about her field (creativity and business), her target audience (corporations, government agencies, and entrepreneurs), how she stands out (PhD, government task force, business application of psychological skills), and why she is in the business (because she has a lifelong passion for creativity and see its relevance in the modern world). What could be improved are the length and complexity of the sentences; when the speech is read aloud, the long, complex sentences are easy to stumble over. As you craft a two-minute version of your own story, try to hit similar content points but break them up into shorter, simpler sentences.

The other element that cannot be ignored about a speech is the presentation of the content. Is the person making eye contact? Is he allowing for appropriate pauses between sentences or rushing from one thought to the next? Dos she use gestures, or is she stiff? Is he inflecting his voice or raising and lowering the volume at appropriate places to convey emotion and keep it interesting for the listener? Does the presentation feel authentic, or forced and overly rehearsed? You may have the best content in the world, but if the presentation component of the APB isn't showing up, the words of your elevator speech will translate more like elevator music. After you draft your text, be sure to practice it in front of the mirror or with a friend to maximize its effectiveness.

## Your Story: Long Version

The fifteen-minute version of your story dives deep into the key facets of your adaptive professional brand. It is what you use when a person in your target market invites you into the office to sit down for a few minutes. This version of your story should make an irrefutable case for you as a professional and be the most irresistible display of the services you provide. It should also anticipate and answer the most vital question that can be posed to a professional:

"Why you?"

The two little words that make up this question—which is the third key question—are packed with subtexts that go way below their surface meaning:

- "Why should I be talking to you right now?"
- "Why should I give you the promotion?"
- "Why should you get the job?"
- "Why should you earn my business?"
- "Why do you deserve this opportunity more than someone else?"

The fifteen-minute version of your story should be crafted to meet and answer these and other versions of the "Why you?" question.

Unlike the two-minute version of your story, this version is meant to be more of a dialogue with the listener. Talking for fifteen minutes straight about yourself and your value is one sure way to lose your audience and whatever opportunity they bring with them.

Instead of drafting an entire speech for this more dynamic presentation of your story, you should outline a set of clear talking points that you can work into the dialogue at any opportunity. The best way to identify these points is to go back through your APB diagnostic survey and focus on two or three pieces of information from each APB component (presentation, offering, mission), with which you will be able to confidently respond to any of the likely "Why you?" subtext questions. I recommend that these focus points include facets of brand name recognition (high-profile schools, clients, or employers), skills and experience, mission, and a few "fun facts" people might not know about you as a professional (like unique certifications, awards, or languages you speak). For each point ask yourself, "How does this component or piece of information communicate why I am the best choice for my employer (or job prospect, or client)? And what does it say about my adaptive professional brand?"

Your answer to "Why you?" doesn't all have to be about how you are better, stronger, or faster than your competition. As we learned from our friends the finches, "Why you?" should also be about the minute variations and unique combinations of APB components that make you compelling. The nuances of variation and differentiation are what survival of the fittest is all about, not blunt aggression and domination.

## break it down: your brand statement

With these three keys in mind—"What's your tagline?" "What's your story?" and "Why you?"—I'd like you to take some time to answer the following questions as a way to solidify your APB:

- How can you describe your APB in fifteen words or less (your tagline)?
- How can you describe your APB in two minutes (your elevator speech)?

- What components and highlights will you touch on in your longer brand story?
- What does your brand promise your target market?
- Can you explain in two to four sentences why your employer, job prospect, or client should choose you over anyone else?

One of the things I found most helpful when I was working on my own APB a few years ago was writing down answers to the above questions and then condensing them into a one-paragraph brand statement. It was written in the first person, using simple language. I printed out that statement and keep it posted above my computer monitor as a reminder to myself of my professional story, my worth, and my differentiation. I see it almost every day when I sit down to work, and it reminds me to leverage my mission and communicate it to my target market. I have found it invaluable, and I recommend you do something similar. Here's mine:

*My name is Nacie Carson, and I am a professional development author and career evolutionist. My professional mission is to provide thoughtful, inspiring, and action-provoking content of the highest quality and integrity to American professionals interested in professional evolution, authenticity, and entrepreneurship. My passion for this work comes from my own experience as a young professional trying to find her way in the workforce and build a career that is fulfilling, successful, and supportive of my personal values. The promise I make to my target market is the presentation and explanation of both accurate and mission-driven strategies for directing and building a career, and I deliver on this promise by focusing and blending business and lifestyle with equal weight.*

I shared some of these APB exercises with Emily, whom you met earlier in this chapter. The questions came at an interesting time in her career, as she was in transition from not just one job to another but one industry to another. After four years working in support and marketing positions at a global healthcare management and solutions firm, she started working as a producer for a boutique postproduction company that specializes in creative editorial for advertising and cinema. When she encountered my material, her challenge was to separate her brand from her organization and to craft an APB that can travel with her through different roles and industries over the life of her career. In reflecting on her experience working on her APB, she made a comment that I think summarizes the entire branding experience perfectly:

"If you'd asked me what my professional brand was a year ago, I might've said my brand is focused on helping improve access to and quality of healthcare in the US and abroad. But having recently changed careers entirely, your questions forced me to think about what *my* brand is, and what traits and professional skills make me valuable to both companies. The cornerstones of my brand are creativity, hard work, resourcefulness, and positive thinking. I thrive in situations that challenge me to solve a problem without experience or preparation—I enjoy educating myself on the fly and finding a solution that fits the context. I am intuitively a hard worker, so finding a solution always motivates me to find another—I don't stop when one job is done; I look ahead to see what else can be done to improve things for the future. Believing anything is possible and that no job is too small comes intuitively to me. As I mature and grow professionally, I'd like to continue to reevaluate and define my brand in a way that stays true to who I am but also helps guide my professional direction in a way that makes me happy."

Well said, Emily. However, being able to communicate and project our brand is only the way to *package* our professional value and differentiation. In order to really *leverage* them, we need to have the confidence and capability to deliver on the promise of our adaptive professional brand. Are you ready to work up a skill-strengthening sweat?

# 4

# cultivate your skills

To this point, the Finch Effect has called upon you to focus most of your efforts on intellectual and theoretical strategies, including adopting the gig mindset and building your professional brand. These strategies have kept your efforts in the realm of perspective, the element that accounts for 90 percent of evolutionary success. Now with the third strategy of the Finch Effect, we are going to begin to shift our attention away from perception and toward the process of identifying, preparing for, and implementing action. Specifically, this third strategy explores the actions you can take to cultivate your skills.

Even though action is only 10 percent of what allows our careers to evolve, it is an essential 10 percent. It comprises polishing existing skills and acquiring needed new ones, as well as letting go of behaviors or habits that hold us back. In a precarious job market, all of us can stand to improve and upgrade our professional skill sets, whether we are at the top of our industry or just starting our careers. In times such as these, all professionals are on call to play beyond their "A-game" in order to maintain control of their careers and communicate a stellar adaptive professional brand. Having a skill set that is up to date and continually polished puts you in a position to take advantage of a great gig opportunity, parlay that part-time job into a full-time position, move strategically within your organization, or approach the job search with confidence.

In terms of the Finch Effect, cultivating your skills is not just about nurturing skills you want to improve but also about managing and releasing counterproductive habits or behaviors that interfere with the communication or delivery of your adaptive professional brand. We are all made up of professional virtues and vices—even the most accomplished among us—and the goal of this strategy is to highlight the virtues and downplay the vices.

## promise and delivery

It is important to cultivate your skills so that your adaptive professional brand (APB) accurately reflects your capabilities and skills to your target market. Disappointing employers, clients, and customers by promising one thing but delivering something much less can derail your career. We've all seen it happen with highly paid sports stars, much-anticipated movies, and politicians who can't live up to their campaign buzz. But it can happen to people outside of the spotlight as well.

When it comes to surviving in the job market of tomorrow, members of the Fittest know it isn't enough to talk a big game about how you are better than your competition and package it all in impressive branding. You have got to be able to deliver on the promise of your differentiation to your target market.

As you are considering the branding questions from the previous chapter, it's easy to start envisioning a totally new professional you . . . and that vision can easily run away with itself if you are not careful.

And herein lies the challenging part: there is *meant* to be an aspirational element to your brand. I mentioned that incorporating aspirations into my APB helped me select opportunities that supported those goals. However, you have to take care that only a few choice elements of your brand are aspirational and that you clearly communicate to members of your target market what skills are current and what are "upcoming." Obviously, I couldn't tell people I was a published author when I wasn't. That would have been false advertising, a brand killer in any market. But I could and did tell them I was working toward being published, thus truthfully leveraging that component of my brand.

Let me share with you an example of overpromising and underdelivering gone wrong. My first real job was working as a hostess and sometime waitress at Bickford's, a breakfast-anytime restaurant in Hanover, Massachusetts. Sure, the food was subpar at best and the clientele was predominantly made up of the elderly and butt-pinching truckers (an interesting mix, I assure you), but it was the only place I could work. I really wanted to work at the Italian restaurant up the street but couldn't, because at 17 I wasn't old enough to serve alcohol.

So I set my sights on Bickford's, and pleaded with the manager to give me a chance over the other kids looking for summer work. "I can do it all," I promised her as she eyed my job application skeptically. "I can deal with customers, manage the register, and wait tables. Please give me a chance!"

My term of employment there was little better than a disaster. I was overwhelmed with just about every portion of my job, from making the coffee to dealing with customers. My then-boyfriend even liked to joke about how I turned my hostess responsibilities—which consisted of a simple section rotation—into a confusing, flustering problem. When I left at the end of the summer, my manager made it clear that I shouldn't bother coming back until I could perform simple tasks, like brewing the coffee properly. Ouch . . .

I share this shame with you to illustrate how failing to deliver on your hype about why you are the best choice for a job or contract is the fastest way to go extinct. And keep in mind that my breakfast-joint fiasco occurred a decade ago. In the current job climate, the horrendous review my Bickford's manager would give to my next employer would have been a vocational death sentence. (Thank the gods for compelling teacher referrals.)

If you are going to include aspirational elements in your APB—which I do recommend—you need to use them as an immediate call to action to improve your skills. This is what cultivating your skills is all about. The implementation of this strategy requires a two-pronged approach that will have you first improve the top five to seven skills you outlined during your APB diagnostics—these are your *differentiating skills*— and then choose just one of them to refine and showcase as your *centerpiece skill*. Upgrading the skills you outlined in your APB will help you not only have the courage of your vocational convictions but also earn more attention from your target market, whether you are reaching out to current employers, future employers, or clients.

One of my favorite examples of how cultivating your skills can make all the difference in achieving your spot among the

Fittest is Mary Beth. As an unemployed freelance writer, Mary Beth knew she had to stand out from myriad other writers fighting for the same opportunities. So she joined a local writer's club in Rhode Island to improve her writing skill set. On a whim she hired a tech-savvy neighborhood kid to teach her how to write iPhone apps. "I had dabbled with some programming in the past, but nothing too formal," Mary Beth notes. It wasn't until a prospective client brought it up that Mary Beth realized the potential of being able to write apps. "It's a rather unusual accomplishment to have on the résumé, and somehow it intrigued clients because they themselves want to produce, write, and sell apps," she notes.

The $20 an hour she paid her neighbor to help her refine her app skills paid off and eventually helped her land a six-month trial contract with a small insurance agency in Pennsylvania. "It was great to go into an interview and say, 'Let me show you my app on my iPhone . . . ' Having that kind of proof of my skill was really helpful."

The skill that Mary Beth chose to highlight as her centerpiece skill became clear to her in a flash of inspiration. But for the rest of us, figuring out where to put our time, money, and effort in perfecting our skills can be a little more confusing, right?

Not really; at least not if you are paying attention to the finches.

## exceptional to the rule

When it comes to surviving in the age of vocational Darwinism, being a member of the Fittest requires you to bring your differentiating skills up to snuff, then pick just one to make your crown jewel centerpiece skill. Choosing one exceptional element is an easy way to elevate your entire brand to wow-worthy status.

The fact is that we don't need to be exceptional at *all* the skills we outline as our differentiators: one is all it takes to push us over the threshold from just surviving to being able to flourish. In fact, niche exceptionalism is a key facet of evolution. Most of the species on the planet today have survived not because of an ability to be awesome at everything but because of their ability to be exceptional at just one (maybe two) things.

Think about Darwin's finches: those little birds are not particularly exceptional at flight, and they don't have very colorful feathers. But they are pretty fantastic at finding new ways to get their dinner (pulling larvae out of tiny holes in the rock, digging into cactuses), and as we know by now, those skills have made all the difference in their ability to thrive.

In the professional food chain, it's the same. Having one exceptional skill, supported by other *pretty good* skills, can help you earn your membership as one of the Fittest. The most obvious examples of this fact include the media moguls and celebrities that fill our pop-culture minds: Oprah, David Beckham, and Martha Stewart all have exceptional skills (show hosting, soccer playing, homemaking) that are supported by other, pretty good skills (savvy marketing know-how, writing ability, product promotion, and so on). The combination of those two distinct types of skills has not only rocketed those individuals to fame and fortune but kept them on top for a decade or more.

We lowly members of the masses can also use this two-pronged approach of (1) improving our skills and (2) exceptionalizing them for our own survival. Take Jamie, for example. Jamie knew he was always going to be lost in the crowd of outside salespeople at the midsized dietary-supplement company he worked for. Nothing about his modest sales skill set stood out. When he was one of the first to be laid off after the financial crisis, his vocational mediocrity became unavoidably obvious. The time had come to stand out from his peers or sink like a stone.

After spending some time brushing up on his basic pitch, cold calling, and lead qualifying skills—his competitive differentiators—he decided to add a unique extra skill to his résumé: he earned an associate's degree in web design from an online university. Eighteen months and two website prototypes later, he found a new supplement company that really dug his plan to develop his own product sales websites catering to each of the specific demographics of his selling radius. "They were pleased with my skill set in general, but were really sold on my ability to make high-quality web pages that spoke directly to the different kinds of people in this area the products are suited for. If I didn't find something to be really exceptional in, I would probably still be job-hunting with everyone else."

## differentiating skills: step up your game

When you think back on the five to seven skills you outlined as part of your APB, what kind of a grade would you give yourself on them?

There are times in life when it is appropriate to B.S. yourself (like how you handled the news that your ex was getting married). This is not one of those times. Overestimating your talent or skill proficiency will land you where

I was, with a snaggletoothed high school dropout boss mocking your inability to handle elderly pancake-eaters. Or something like that.

This is a time for honesty and self-awareness. Even if you don't have a habit of denial, it is very important that you reach out to your friends or trusted colleagues and ask them to help you complete this exercise. We're talking survival of the fittest here, and self-deception is counterproductive to your survival and your fitness. I've developed a diagnostic to help you grade your differentiating skills. I use it myself to grade my work at The Life Uncommon, and I always ask a handful of friends, fellow professionals, and readers for their input to ensure I am getting the most accurate picture.

Before you can work on your centerpiece skill (though you can certainly be thinking about it now), you need to assess your other differentiating skills so that you can step up those that are lacking. Here is a sample of the skill scorecard I use personally, and with the people I work with, to get a snapshot of what needs improvement. You can download a blank template with room for up to ten skills at TheLife Uncommon.net.

As you can see, the scorecard is pretty easy to fill in: simply list each of the competitive differentiating skills in the left column, give each one a grade, elaborate on why you chose that grade, and then identify how to upgrade the skill. If you are employing other people to rate you on these skills, I recommend giving them all their own sheets and then compiling those sheets into a master grid, listing the average score.

Once you have used this scorecard to get a descriptive picture of your proficiency in each of your differentiating skills,

| Differentiating Skill | Skill Proficiency Grade (1 = non-existent, 10 = expert) | Elaboration on Grade | Needed Upgrades |
|---|---|---|---|
| People management | 8 | I can usually get a team to do what I need them to do, but have problems with encounter | — |
| Professional networking | 5 | I can sometimes make great connections, and other times have no idea how to reach out to people | Improve conversation skills, improve confidence in swapping business cards and leaving people open to working together later on |
| Product promotion with social media | 6 | Using social media is not an issue, but balancing the right tone and promotion strategy is challenging | Identify appropriate promotional tone and product placement frequency, types of links shared |

you can identify which ones need attention and brainstorm what to do about them.

In my experience, you shouldn't spend too much of your time improving skills that are at a grade of 7 or above. While the perfectionist in me cringes to hear this (obviously, if it isn't a 10, it isn't good enough!), the realist in me knows that time and resources are limited and therefore need to be selectively employed. Skills that are at a 7 are skills that are in pretty good shape, and really, that is just where they need to be for now. Employers, clients, and customers will feel satisfied if they find you proficient and capable in these areas and can forgive small imperfections. If you have a burning desire later to update those skills, by all means go ahead. But at this stage of the strategy, embrace your 7+'s and shift your focus onto the mediocre skills.

As for those other, under-7 skills, they need to be whipped into shape pronto. You run the risk of professionally failing to deliver on your personal brand if you are simply average or below average on your differentiating skills. But how do you get them up to snuff?

The equation is mercifully simple: look at the needed upgrades, brainstorm ways you could accomplish them, and then analyze their cost. Let's break this down a little.

## brainstorming skill upgrades

In my talks with members of the Fittest, I've noticed that the ways they upgrade their flagging skills fall into a handful of basic categories:

- *Self-taught* (online research, how-to guides, practice, trial and error)
- *Informal apprenticeships or training* (learning from working with someone who is proficient in the skill)
- *Formal training* (typically resulting in a degree, certification, internship, fellowship, or license)

These three categories also happen to be listed in order of general cost (though specific cost would depend on your specific industry). Let me take a minute to review what I mean by the word "cost." You have three major resources available to you: your time, your energy, and your money. When I refer to cost, I mean a combination of all three of these things. An example of a low-cost endeavor is something that requires minimal time, energy, or money—like buying a self-help book and reading it. An example of a high-cost endeavor is getting your MBA, an undertaking that requires tens of thousands of dollars and several years of energy.

Here are two great examples of how the skill upgrade categories look in action:

Wayne started a web-based company focused on helping people be happier in their jobs. Because his company was a side project to his day job, Wayne needed to find a low-cost way to upgrade his differentiating skills. Before he launched his business, he told me that he "read every marketing and networking website online, as well as every published paper and book on online businesses. I even contacted and interviewed each book author to learn as much as possible." Using this self-taught/informal-apprenticeship approach, Wayne was able to bring his marketing, networking, and online business skills from 2, 6, and 4, respectively, to 7+'s in a matter of months.

Colin also wanted to open a web-based business, and chose online advertising for his business focus. When it came to bringing up his differentiating skills to an acceptable level, he tried several different tactics. First he got his master's certificate in online marketing from the University of San Francisco. "It cost me six thousand dollars and was pretty good, but not a great choice for the money and time I had to spend on it," he recalls. Colin found more benefit from two other skill upgrading strategies: utilizing online tutorials to master Apple video editing software, and learning the inner workings of Google

AdWords. He also found a site, Lynda.com, that offered a variety of online courses for under $40 a month. "This was the best place for cranking up my skills. It was a big help."

These two examples might lead you to believe I don't recommend formal education or training as a way to upgrade your skill strategies. That inference would be partly right. Many professionals today are flocking to advanced degree programs for lack of a better plan; however, this course of action can land you thousands of dollars in debt and with a degree that doesn't really make much of a difference in your vocational future. I don't support the "I'll get a degree so I can feel like I am going somewhere" mentality; it is wasteful and counterproductive, two things that are the antithesis of how the Fittest behave. Of course, there are exceptions: some fields, such as accounting, medical practice, or law, may require some advancement of degree to enter a higher level of opportunity. But when you start to brainstorm ways you can upgrade your differentiating skills, I want you to think about choosing options that are going to give you the *most return for the lowest cost.* If you can improve one of your skills by reading a book instead of taking a semester-long class somewhere, then my vote would be for the book. (Note that our strategy will be a bit different when it comes to your exceptional skill. But for your other differentiating skills, conserving personal cost is important.)

As you consider your options for upgrading your differentiating skills, think about asking people you know who are good at them how they got to their level of competency. When I built my first website in 2008, my first instinct was to pay for a set of online seminars that covered the basics. However, when I asked a friend of mine how he figured out how to build his site, he directed me to an exhaustive (and free!) online guide

## upgrade differentiating skills

The best way to brainstorm your options for upgrading your under-7 differentiating skills is to think about your options within the three categories (self-taught, informal, formal). Here are some basic questions to ask that can help you outline your choices:

- What websites focus on this skill?
- What books provide how-to instruction on this skill, and how much do they cost?
- Whom do I know, personally or through connections, that is proficient at this skill?
- What classes are available (online and off-line) that teach this skill, how long are they, and what do they cost?

First answer these questions off the top of your head, and then do a Google search for each to come up with additional solutions. Amazon.com works for a comprehensive book search.

that taught me all I needed to know. That gave me an extra $150 to spend on other things, like stock photos, software, and a newsletter service. Sweet.

Getting your differentiating skills up to snuff is essential to joining the ranks of the Fittest. It's all good, whether you choose to pick up a book, read a website, or apprentice yourself to your neighbor's uncle's friend who is great at a particular skill. It is vital to keep an eye on your personal cost, because you are going to need to save all your extra resources—time, energy, and money—to hit a home run with your centerpiece skill.

## break it down: reaching out to experts

A great strategy to help develop your skills is to seek out an industry expert for an informational interview. If you know (or know of) anyone who has mastered the kind of skill you are working on, then try to reach out to them via e-mail. There is no better way to ascertain what you need to do (and don't need to do) to get started than to talk to someone who has already been there. You shouldn't feel shy about asking—most people are only too happy to share their experiences with someone else. Such people will also turn into great contacts for you as you continue in the field.

If you are attempting to contact someone you don't know, use this model for drafting an introductory e-mail:

Dear So-and-So,

My name is [insert name] and I have been interested in [or a fan of] your work for quite some time. I am working on my [insert skill] and was wondering if you would be available sometime to chat about it with me for a few minutes, and allow me to ask some questions about your experiences mastering this skill. I would be very grateful! I am free at your leisure, and look forward to talking to you!

Many thanks,

## your centerpiece skill: mastering perfection

When you think about your centerpiece skill, your crown jewel, what you are really thinking about is what you want to be known for. This is the skill that will be played up in your tagline and attached to your name at all opportunities through your adaptive professional brand. I've always made writing my centerpiece skill because I love to do it and am proud of my capabilities. Mary Beth strategically made writing iPhone applications her centerpiece skill to add a unique element to her résumé. Jim Carrey chose ridiculous facial expressions as his crown jewel and has been cast in over forty films and counting as a result.

What you choose to be your centerpiece should be something in which you are confident you can be exceptional—and I don't just mean pretty good or noteworthy; I mean industry-leading exceptional. When you feature this skill to employers or clients, you need to do so with the utmost confidence that should they hire you or purchase this skill, they will get more than their money's worth. If they don't, then they know there are plenty of other professionals out there who are dying for the chance to deliver on their brand promises, making you, in a word, expendable. And you need to be able to deliver right from the gate; the Fittest know that they need to establish their proficiency and worth immediately or risk getting pushed down the food chain.

This is why the rules of cost and benefit are different for this one skill compared to your other differentiating skills. While with your other competitive differentiators it is acceptable to have a grade of 7 or above, your centerpiece skill needs to be at minimum a 9, and preferably a 10. This is where impressive credentials, extensive training, and considerable time practicing and cultivating your skills come into play. Instead of looking for an upgrade that will get you the most output for the least input, you need to consider upgrade options that will get you the most impact, whatever it takes. MBAs, CPAs, fellowships, certifications, apprenticeships with industry leaders: all are fair to be considered for upgrading your centerpiece skill.

So how do you choose this one awesome "calling card" skill from your list of competitive differentiators? It should match at least two of these three criteria:

- It is already graded a 9 or 10 on your skill scorecard
- You love to do it
- You have the time, energy, and financial budget to get it to a 9 or 10

Let me explain these criteria further.

One thing that stands out when you look at the survival of a species is how the conservation of resources is always involved. It typically takes a massive shift in external forces or conditions to cause members of a species to stop doing something they are exceptional at in favor of doing something new. For example, some finches are exceptional at eating specific types of larva. They wouldn't suddenly start to eat some other kind of food because they felt like it; that would take resources away from other vital functions. The only thing that would get the finches to pursue a different food source would be the inability to eat larvae anymore.

Likewise, when it comes to your centerpiece skill, it makes little sense to pursue another option when you are already exceptional at something. Why would you spend thousands of dollars to become great at an instrument you don't even play instead of highlighting your concert-level piano skills? That would be a poor use of valuable time, energy, and money.

A poor use, yes, unless you have a burning passion to play another instrument and couldn't care less about the piano. Hence the second criterion. Whatever you choose as your centerpiece skill should be something you like to do, because it is going to be a foundational factor in your professional survival for the foreseeable future. Furthermore, employers and clients get a better product when it comes from a place of personal interest and investment, because you are willing to go that extra mile. I am actually quite fantastic at budget management (and also, incidentally, cleaning countertops), but I don't really enjoy doing it. I would much rather feature my writing, something I love doing, as my centerpiece skill, even though it requires constant updating and enhancement.

The third and final criterion for choosing your crown jewel is whether or not you have the time, energy, and financial support to get the skill to exceptional levels. In all honesty, I've always had an interest in making people management a centerpiece skill, but I haven't been able to invest the time or energy into taking this skill to a 9 or 10. Since I am naturally at about a 3 or 4 with this skill, I would quickly go extinct if I promised employers the ability to manage people exceptionally and then couldn't deliver. It would be Bickford's all over again, on a bigger, more disastrous scale.

Once you pick your centerpiece, it is just a matter of revisiting the upgrade brainstorming questions and choosing the options that will get you to exceptional in the most effective way possible. Our friend Jamie had the idea to feature web design as one of his differentiating skills after he heard about another salesman in a different field increasing his numbers by 125 percent by building demographic-specific sites. As Jamie started to forge a new professional future in the first part of the Finch Effect, he realized that incorporating web design into his sales plan could be powerful, as well as being underutilized by others. So web development was bumped from differentiating skill to centerpiece skill: "I knew that in order to make this skill worthwhile, I had to be able to build high-quality, professional-grade sites." After reviewing the options for getting this skill—which he initially graded 2 on his scorecard—to a 9 or 10, Jamie decided that an online degree program would give him the most comprehensive experience and exposure to the latest trends. His energy in the program paid off, and the proof is in the pudding: his demographic-specific website sales plan is setting a new standard for sales channels at his company.

## managing counterproductive behaviors

While the main focus of this chapter is on helping you cultivate a set of skills to bolster your adaptive professional brand, we need to take a few minutes to review what behaviors or habits you might have that are working *against* the success of your adaptive professional brand and your skill development so that you can neutralize their impact.

A quick point: no matter what these habits are, you shouldn't feel ashamed, embarrassed, or angered by them. Everyone—even celebrities, Fortune 100 business leaders, and spiritual leaders—has idiosyncrasies, which can run the gamut from barely negligible offenses to quirks that a target market would notice and potentially take issue with. The goal is not to turn you into some kind of Stepford-like professional but instead to make you mindful of how you might be unknowingly working against all the hard work you have done on this and the preceding strategies, and to give you an opportunity to adjust accordingly.

To start identifying these counterproductive habits, you are once again going to reach out to people who are close to you to solicit feedback on your interactive habits. The truth is that we are just about blind to many of our own bad habits. For example, when I was growing up, I said "um" and "like" frequently in my conversations. I only remember that I did this because my father pulled me aside one day and said he was going to make a discreet signal at the dinner table—a tug on his ear—every time I added those fillers in the pauses of my sentences so that I could see exactly how often I did it. You can imagine that by the time dinner was over his ear was bright red and he was deflecting questions from my perplexed mother as to whether he had something wrong with his ear.

The sore ear was worth the effort: as soon as I was aware of the habit, I began to correct it, and today I can safely tell you my conversations are free of "ums" and "likes." I didn't realize how valuable that awareness of my word fillers was until I was at a professional event where the speaker was an "um-er" and I heard the disparaging, sidelong comments people were making about it. Thanks, Dad!

## break it down: getting feedback on your habits

Just like the content of self-talk, much of what you'll find in the responses you receive to this brief survey is correctable as soon as you become mindful of the habit. Below are the key questions you will pass on to someone who has observed you interacting with others lately. Observation of interaction in a professional capacity is preferable, but in school or at home is better than nothing. When soliciting this feedback, ask for genuine, honest responses. Let your responders know how much you appreciate their insights and candor.

- How would you describe the way I verbally communicate? Do I swear, use sentence fillers, or vocalize my comments in too bombastic or too meek a manner? Do I cut people off, mumble, or stutter in my responses?
- What can you observe about my physical presentation that I should be aware of? Do my dress, posture and carriage, physical neatness, and hygiene meet your standards of professionalism?
- Do I use any unconscious and repetitive phrases or actions that other people become quickly aware of (a foot tap, or repeating "you know")?
- Could you offer any other candid feedback about any behaviors or habits I display in interacting with others that could compromise my presentation or distract from my brand as a professional?

When you receive the responses to these questions, read them over and check their validity against how you see yourself. If something doesn't resonate with you as being accurate, I want you to write it down on an index card or type it into your smartphone and keep it in your pocket as you go through your typical day. At the end of the day, reread the feedback and take stock of its validity again. If it still doesn't resonate with you, you can set it aside and practice feeling gratitude for the responder's effort. However, if upon review the feedback does make more sense, then congratulations: you are now aware of a habit and have the power to do something about it. As I said earlier, just being mindful of habits like these is typically enough to correct them.

While physical and interactive habits are most easily observed by others, there are many counterproductive behaviors or habits that only we are aware of. These include work habits, lifestyle habits, or self-care habits that negatively influence not necessarily how we interact with others but how we accomplish what we want to in the realm of skill and brand development.

The key question you need to ask yourself is:

*What am I prone to doing or not doing that interferes (or has the potential to interfere) with my ability to achieve the skill development plan I outlined in this chapter within the time frame I want to achieve it?*

Some very common answers to this question include, but certainly are not limited to:

- *Poor time management*: I am not good at effectively managing my schedule to make room for my brand development or skill development
- *Inadequate self-care*: I don't have the mental or emotional resources available to address all the demands on my time at work and at home; I am already frazzled, overwhelmed, and in desperate need of a manicure I have no time to get
- *Problems with follow-through*: I am very good at outlining strategies or action steps but struggle with following through on my plans or seeing them to completion; as a result, I have many half-finished personal and professional development projects
- *Poor work/life balance*: I can barely balance my obligations at work (or school) with my social life as it is; I am either too socially focused to get my work done, or too work focused to enjoy a social life
- *Lost drive*: After initially starting a skill development program, I lose interest, get bored, feel unmotivated, or don't see the point

- *Development skepticism*: I am comfortable with where all my skills are and don't think investing in upgrading them is worth it; I've got it all figured out

## break it down: problem-solving counterproductive tendencies

Take some time to think the above question over before responding to it; try to be mindful as you go through your day of where these internal interferences might occur. Once you have given it some thought, make a list in one column on the left side of a piece of paper of as many elements as you can think of that have the potential to interfere with the development or implementation of your APB or corresponding skills. In the right column, write a response to the following question for each entry:

*Knowing that I [struggle with] [am aware of] this behavior or habit and its potential impact on my professional development, what one or two steps can I take this week to overcome it?*

So, for example, if you listed "poor time management" in the left column as a habit that you can anticipate will interfere with your ability to implement your development plans, then you might put something like "use my Google Calendar more" or "set an alarm to help me keep tasks to a specific time frame" in the right column.

I believe strongly that the act of identifying your potential challenges, and then drafting your own response to those challenges, is the best way to prepare yourself for roadblocks in your skill development. It's also the best way to reinforce your capacity to handle those issues and own the solutions. However, if you include any concerns about follow-through or commitment in your list of counterproductive behaviors, then I will make one suggestion: employ the buddy system. Many development and goal-oriented programs out there are built for people who struggle with follow-through, and all of them employ an accountability system to keep participants in check. Think about Weight Watchers: what really makes that program stand out from other diets and continue to be successful is that it has you weigh in before each weekly meeting. As someone who has used Weight Watchers in the past and found it effective, I can tell you that one of the main reasons I stuck to the program and didn't stray was because I knew there was going to be someone whom I would have to look in the eyes at the end of the week and share my weight with, whether I'd gained or lost.

As you work toward upgrading your differentiating and centerpiece skills, I suggest you find a "buddy"—it can be your supervisor, your spouse, your friend, or your priest—whom you will check in with and be accountable to on a regular basis about your progress. Be sure you empower this person to give you a little talking to if you fall off track!

You will also want to be sure this person is in it for the long haul. In working in personal and professional development for the last three years, I can tell you that skill development is never really finished, at least not if you do it right.

Most people approach skill development with the idea that they will learn the skill, master it, and then move on with their life. Yet in an ever changing, ever evolving world, such a once-and-done attitude not only is unrealistic but also sets you up for failure before you even start. It's unrealistic to imagine that you will ever close the book on the development of a particular skill. This is because of the constant flow and sharing of newer technologies, better strategies, more efficient tools, and more highly trained experts that our globalized economy and enhanced communication systems have helped to create. Additionally, you are in a constant state of change and growth yourself, so what worked for you at one point in your career might not prove as effective even a short time later. This happens incredibly frequently in the context of skills that utilize the latest technologies (think of Mary Beth and her iPhone apps).

But there is a larger message. Members of the Fittest understand that the work they are doing through the Finch Effect strategies doesn't lead to a final destination but is a career-long journey requiring constant attentiveness and care. In the first strategy, you took on the mantle of ownership for your career, and with it you accepted the responsibility for tending it regularly to help it flourish in any economy. Skill development is such a powerful element of your professional evolution that you need to embrace it as a constant throughout your career, or you will set yourself up for failure. The antithesis of adaptation is stasis and lack of change. Members of the Fittest are all about adaptation.

I'll admit, the idea of carrying these strategies for the rest of your career can be an almost overwhelming concept. After all, depending on your age, that could mean another forty to fifty years of focusing on skill development and implementation—I can see how the prospect might cause some fatigue. You can take some hopeful comfort in that you won't necessarily be working on the same specific skills for the duration of your career—although some people do. The skills we focus on improving will change and grow with us as our prowess increases and we take on new roles. The trick is to keep your motivation, goals, and accomplishments all within view to help you keep perspective. Why are you motivated to be a member of the Fittest in the first place? Is it because you want to provide for your family in any economy, or because you have a specific passion you want to pursue as your career? What are your current goals, and what goals have you accomplished?

As members of the Fittest, we are responsible for putting our own carrot in front of our own horse. Classically, the best way to do that is through a clear understanding of where you have been, where you are going, and why.

## setting the wheels in motion

If you are anything like me, your schedule is stuffed to the gills. This is why setting a calendar for skill upgrades has made such a difference in my ability to actually accomplish them. Penciling in time to read that book, or call that expert, or sign up for that class has proven very effective in helping me turn my under-7s into 7+'s so I can confidently go forth and live up to the hype of my adaptive professional brand. You might find other strategies that work better for you; the point is to actively employ *something* to help you build these upgrades into your daily life. I've collected a small library of tools and tricks from members of the Fittest on effectively maintaining your plans to cultivate your skills; these include time-management strategies, budget tips, resource-analysis spreadsheets, and failure-proof ways to confidently reach out to any expert or skill guru for mentorships and interviews. I've uploaded them onto TheLifeUncommon.net so you can access them anytime. Simply log in to The Fittest members-only section to check them out and start setting the wheels in motion.

As you begin to implement your plans for skill development, I encourage you to be patient with yourself and the process. Change and real development take time, no matter what you do to try to speed up results. In his revolutionary

1995 book, *Changing for Good*, James O. Prochaska and his team outlined their six-stage model for how to effectively change behavior. In their model, three out of the six stages focus on mentally preparing for action (precontemplation, contemplation, and preparation); only one stage is devoted to the real act of implementing change (action). The warning is that if you rush through the first three stages of mental preparation for change, you will be unable to effectively implement the act of changing, or—arguably worse—you'll be unable to sustain the change in the "maintenance" stage. On his website, Prochaska notes: "Research has shown that up to 80% of people are not ready to go to action right away. It's something they have to work up to, and not everyone moves at the same pace."[1] So as you move into this new stage of your professional evolution, remember that you have been building up to it through the last several strategies. You have complete power over what steps you take, and when. If it takes you two days or two months to start implementing your skill development plans, then so be it. Move at your own pace so that when you get to the action stage you are ready to dig in and start producing results.

Being confident in your skills and knowing that you have the capability to not just talk the talk but walk the walk will reflect in your current endeavors as well as in the projection of your APB. Confidence has that funny way of ringing through all communication, even digital communication. As soon as you upgrade your differentiating skills and get your centerpiece skill to an exceptional level, you can start getting out there to promote your adaptive professional brand.

And in our modern world, some of the best places to communicate that brand start with three little w's . . .

# 5

# nurture your social network

A re you ready for me to blow your mind?
As of September 2011, there were 750 million Facebook accounts (personal and business pages), and over 225 million of them were registered to Americans. To give you a little perspective, the 2010 US Census counted the population of America at around 312 million people. That means that as many as 72 percent of Americans have registered Facebook accounts. If Facebook statistics are correct that 50 percent of all users log on at least once a day, then as many as 112 million Americans access their account on any given day.[1]

And that is just Facebook. While no other social media site has that large of a user population, Twitter and LinkedIn pull pretty impressive numbers on their own, each boasting over 100 million registered users, numbers that are climbing at a substantial pace.

In a May 2010 interview with the *Daily Mirror*, the singer Prince told the reporter that he was refusing to market his new album online because "The internet's completely over . . . [it's] like MTV. At one time, MTV was hip and suddenly it became outdated."[2]

As much as I hate to argue with a man who told me to party like it was 1999, I have to say that Prince—and anyone else who is resisting the use of social media as a professional tool—is really, really wrong. All you need to do is look at the thousands of new social media accounts being created *every day* around the world to see that the age of the internet isn't over. It's just getting started.

I began my social media career in 2004 when I registered my personal Facebook account. In 2008, I expanded my social media presence to include a Twitter feed and LinkedIn account at the behest of Shawna, a green lifestyle author, blogger, and speaker who advocates better living and improved communities through environmentally friendly practices. I remember talking to Shawna on the phone one afternoon in November 2008 and listening to her explain Twitter. "Really, Nacie, it's the next big thing—you have to sign up, it's an amazing way to connect with people!" I told her I would look into it, although I had serious doubts how a microblogging platform that allowed you to submit only 140 characters at a time could do much to connect anything, let alone be the next big thing.

Not long after I took Shawna's advice and signed up for Twitter, I noticed a tweet from her to her followers: "Holy Cow! My name and photo got on CNN today."

Turns out her tweet was modest: she had actually been interviewed about pet allergies for a story on then-president-elect Obama's search for a dog. I immediately sent her a private message on Twitter to ask all about the article; CNN.com is a big deal, and I needed the details. She messaged me back a few minutes later with the response: "GUESS WHAT? They found me on TWITTER!!! Called me up and interviewed me! Keep Twittering!!!"

Yet three years later, I stand before you not only as a reformed Twitter believer but also as a believer in most things social media, and for one simple reason: I have observed it to be the most effective, results-generating platform available today to workers for communicating an adaptive professional brand. Since the CNN interview, Shawna has been featured on PBS, ABC News, in the *Chicago Tribune*, and in myriad other television, print, radio, and internet outlets, providing her a platform to share her brand's message with her target market.

In this chapter, you are going to learn how to optimize your social media presence to communicate your APB to your target market and start gaining traction as a member of the Fittest. Now there are no promises that CNN or ABC News will come calling, but I can tell you that you will open up your career to greater opportunity, networking possibilities, and growth potential.

When I started online just a few years ago, most of the individual professionals I knew who were plugged into social media had internet-based businesses, online copywriting businesses, blogs, or an e-store. But within what feels like the blink of an eye (or should I say the poke of a Facebook friend?), social media has opened up and is now relevant to many traditional brick-and-mortar industries, job types, and professionals. John Haydon, a social media strategist for nonprofits, author of the third edition of *Facebook Marketing for Dummies*, and personal social media guru to yours truly, notes that "the ability to use social media is a huge competitive advantage for job seekers" because "employees are now the brand, not a logo, and [employers] will give weight to a candidate who knows how to effectively use social media."[3] John also comments that in particular, social media know-how is becoming increasingly important for customer-facing positions.

There is no escaping it: your future as a member of the Fittest is online. For the purposes of our work together, we are going to focus only on how to leverage your Facebook, Twitter, and LinkedIn accounts. I know there are quite a few other social sites out there (Google+, MySpace, FourSquare), but in my personal experience, and according to what I learned from talking to members of the Fittest, these three sites are where the greatest potential for brand leveraging lies.

Before you start arguing that your Facebook page is for personal use only and doesn't have anything to do with your professional life, think again. Whether you like it or not, what you broadcast on social media is part of what people think about when they consider your professional brand. John Haydon notes it is now common practice for employers to search Facebook and other sites to check if and how job candidates navigate the social media stream. Still not convinced? For a potentially rude awakening, just do an internet search of employers who check Facebook profiles during the hiring process. So you might guess (correctly) that the bad news of this chapter is that you are going to have to take down those pictures of yourself at your cousin's bachelor party. But the good news is that by optimizing the huge reach of social media you will have myriad ways to distinguish yourself, communicate your brand, and develop opportunities in any economy. In the long run, this seriously outweighs the freedom to make status updates that read like lines from a Hunter S. Thompson novel.

If the freedom to goof off on social media is that important to you, I suggest you consider an online alias as a way to digitally get down with your bad self. Sure, you could just hide friends-only content from public viewing by adjusting the security settings on your profiles. But over the last few years, frequent changes in privacy-setting policies on major social media sites have made keeping material behind closed virtual doors an act of constant vigilance, not a set-it-and-forget-it feature. Furthermore, in case you didn't hear, the Library of Congress has started archiving the Twitter feed for posterity; so whatever you post under your handle will be captured for future generations . . . and searchable by any interested party. My advice is to rebrand your pages to support your APB and start using the handle SpongeBobAwesomePants22 (for example) as your secret social media identity for your after-hours shenanigans.[4]

It's true that some have found the right balance of professional and personal elements in the same profile. For example, John Haydon purposely chooses not to separate the two and instead has found benefit from maintaining the balance. "People ultimately buy from other people. I am pretty open about my personal life and often express personal and political beliefs. If people have an issue with who I am then I don't want to work with them. On the flip-side, I've found that I actually attract customers who resonate with who I am."

But for the rest of us who are not social media superheroes, I strongly recommend separating online personas to avoid any regret down the road.

And on that note, welcome to the fourth strategy of the Finch Effect: *Nurture your social network*.

## it's not a tweet; it's a career strategy

For all the buzz around social media, quite a few professionals out there still don't have an active profile on one or all of these three major platforms. If you don't have a Facebook profile, Twitter feed, or LinkedIn account, I strongly recommend that you navigate your web browser to those sites right now and register before reading the rest of this chapter. Registration at all three sites is free.

When I hear that someone, especially someone in the 20–45-year-old range, isn't tweeting, posting, or sharing, I am pretty surprised, if for no other reason than that they obviously don't understand the opportunities they are missing to advance their career. But Crystal understands. In August 2011 she was laid off from her position of three years as director of social media and communications for a Fortune 500 software company. What has kept her afloat and advancing her career in spite of this unfortunate event? Her social media network. "When I was recently laid off, my [social media] network rallied around me, sharing job listings, connecting me with people that they knew and offering moral support. Within a few days I had landed three interviews and lined up two short term contracts to keep me afloat until something permanent comes along. . . . [My social media network] propelled me above the competition when it comes to finding a job in a tough economic climate."

Yet her social media presence was returning rewards long before she was laid off: "Keeping my LinkedIn profile up-to-date means that recruiters call me regularly, at least a few times a month. Twitter has enabled me to correspond with people in my industry including reporters that may be covering stories by companies with whom I am working."

For Crystal, social media has meant much more than just a place to post weekend party pictures or share YouTube videos about cats in fake mustaches (yes, that exists). Social media has not only helped her communicate her adaptive professional brand effectively but also become a way to continue to grow her career. "Social media is a very powerful tool to help you build and shape your reputation. Building a vast social media network primarily means that when I need something, be it the answer to a technical question, a lead on a vendor, a recommendation for new technology, or leads on a job, I have several hundred people I can fall back on."

I share Crystal's perspective: social media provides opportunities, networking possibilities, and branding support that can almost instantaneously start yielding rewards. Thanks to my social network, I have had access to an international stream of writing offers, qualified business opportunities, and moral support over the last several years. In fact, I strongly credit my ability to thrive as a freelancer during a recession to the social network I have cultivated.

One of the most powerful ways my online network has helped me grow as a professional is through the transfer of knowledge and unofficial mentorship. As surreal as it may sound, I can honestly say I have learned most of what I know about career success from people I've never spoken with on the phone or met in person. I haven't even seen a picture of some of them (why people use pictures of their dogs as their profile image I'll never understand). Whether it was through conversations on Facebook or Twitter or just observing them interact with other people through these sites, I was able to figure out how to build and customize the first iterations of my website, write compelling sales copy, allocate my business finances, write a book proposal, and organize my time as a freelancer, all thanks to a digital network of tutors, gurus, and industry leaders.

Developing and maintaining active social media relationships can also contribute to your psychological resilience. In Chapter Two we focused on how resilience, or the ability to adapt in the face of adversity, can help prepare us to adopt the gig mindset and own our careers. One of the ten tactics the American Psychological Association suggests for building resilience is "make connections," because "good relationships with close family members, friends, or others are important. Accepting help and support from those who care about you and will listen to you strengthens resilience. Some people find that being active in civic groups, faith-based organizations, or other local groups provides social support and can help with reclaiming hope. Assisting others in their time of need also can benefit the helper." Many individuals who don't find themselves in civic or local groups can receive the same benefit from community and the same opportunity to give and receive support through their online connections. Who knew that when I was reaching out to other bloggers and sharing stories and support I was also building my resilience?[5]

Members of the Fittest know. They understand how valuable social media can be when cultivated as part of their career evolution strategy, and not simply as a way to track down high school classmates. But should you interact and promote your APB in the same way on each site, or are different sites better for different conversations?

Let's find out.

## where to go for what

With all of their site-specific terminology (tweeting, liking, poking, recommending), each of the three main social media sites we are looking at, as fledgling members of the Fittest, can quickly start feeling confusing, and about as accessible as Klingon. I remember feeling lost in the social media universe myself when I first started. Since I wasn't really clear what each site was supposed to do, I tended to just post the same exact update on all my profiles as a default strategy to appear active. That worked pretty well, until a Facebook friend kindly pointed out that people were noticing, and not in a good way.

Such a mistake is understandable, as the sites have basic similarities: they all allow users to create personal profiles with pictures, connect with other users, view an activity feed populated by people they connect with, send and receive private messages, and manage their account settings. But outside of these elements, each site features different types of conversations, and in very different tones. Members of the Fittest understand that they need to adjust how they communicate their APB—and the part they focus on communicating—according to the specific social media site.

For example, I've observed that most members of the Fittest use Facebook as a way to answer the second APB marketing question, "What is your story?" and to share information that rounds them out as professionals and people. This strategy fits perfectly with Facebook's capabilities as (arguably) the most comprehensive social media platform. In addition to being a very visually focused network (uploading, sharing, and incorporating rich media is super easy), Facebook places no limitations on the amount of content you can share in your status feed. The profile page alone allows you to share an incredible amount of information that can help pull you out of that two-or-three-word-descriptor box we discussed in Chapter Three. You can list everything from what books you like to television shows you watch to quotes you are inspired by to websites you read. Facebook provides an amazingly comprehensive way to communicate the mission and physical presentation components of your APB.

Yet as Sharon Machlis of Computerworld.com noted in a July 2011 piece comparing the various social media sites, "My sense is that Facebook is best either for personal connections or corporate brands and less for connecting with individuals (who aren't celebrities) you don't know personally."[6] Crystal shares a similar opinion and observes that for her, Facebook is more of a personal network than a professional one. But that's not to say she isn't indirectly supporting her APB: "Your [Facebook] friends are going to help you first, so cultivate the personal network so that when you need a referral you have it."

Sharon and Crystal also both agree that the best place to forge more traditional business connections is on LinkedIn. LinkedIn, which bills itself as a professional networking site, not a social media site, is best suited for sharing the offering components of your APB. Crystal uses the site to "manage my main job profile, which serves as a sort of online résumé." Like many LinkedIn users, Crystal takes advantage of the recommendations feature to solicit and display endorsements of her professional prowess; and the status update option to share career-relevant information, such as new employment, awards, or client projects.

One of the interesting facets of LinkedIn is that while your profile can be made public, you are only able to interact with people with whom you have gone to school or done business. If you want to get in touch with someone who is out of your network (say, Kevin Bacon), you can request an introduction through one of your contacts who knows his contacts. The restrictions of your network are meant to enhance the trust factor on the site and make the interaction on the site more impactful and exclusive-feeling.

While the site, as Sharon notes, is trying to "leverage its large user base for something besides career networking," generalized content sharing is not on par with Facebook. At this point, interactions on LinkedIn remain largely based on job and career opportunity.[7]

It might be surprising, but members of the Fittest understand that the best place among these three main social media sites to cultivate new contacts and professional relationships is Twitter. The brevity of 140-character status updates is conducive to dialogue in the same way instant messaging and texting are, allowing readers to grasp the gist of comments or questions quickly and respond in kind. It also makes the sharing of headlines, article titles, and links fast and easy.

Twitter's success, in spite of its curt update format, is due to its lack of boundaries. Unless you specifically block someone, your tweets are all open to anyone who subscribes to your updates (aka "follows you"), checks your profile, or reads the universal Twitter feed. And unless you are specifically blocked, nothing stops you from replying to anyone's tweet, be it your grandmother's or Barack Obama's (yes, he has a Twitter account . . . with over ten million followers). The result is unparalleled access to a whole spectrum of interesting, industry-relevant, and famous people.

For Crystal, Twitter "helps me to connect with individuals in my fields of interest, stay up to date on news and information and to position myself with the audiences I care about." Sharon expressed a similar sentiment in her article, noting that Twitter was "still my preferred platform for finding and following interesting people . . . I am much more likely to follow someone I don't personally know in my Twitter stream."

In my own experience, I have made the majority of my online contacts and relationships through Twitter. When I take a chance and timidly reply to one of my professional heroes online, I am often surprised by how many of them comment back and engage with me for a few tweets. It is truly an egalitarian form of modern communication, and it can be used effectively to promote the paper presentation, offering, and mission components of your APB.

The trick is to involve yourself in conversations on all three of these platforms, and optimize the parameters of each to send a clear message to your target market on all three portals.

## rebranding your social media pages

As the digital presentation component of your APB, your major social media profiles need to:

- project a consistent message of your professional brand
- be tailored to both your target market and the tone and dialogue of the specific social media outlet

To accomplish these two goals it is inevitable that you will need to rebrand each of your social media profiles.

When doing a social media profile rebranding, the best start is always with a good cleaning of any content that you don't want employers, clients, or coworkers to see. A little caveat about deleting a social media post: just because you can't see it on your feed anymore doesn't mean it's truly gone; for example, Google search bots could have catalogued the post already, or a friend could have reposted it on his or her site. The best you can do is to clean up your pages as well as possible and hope nothing comes back to haunt you. If it does, there isn't much you can do about it except let it go and make better posting choices going forward. If you are starting your profiles from scratch, please be sure to read through this section anyway to learn about and hopefully avoid the common social media pitfalls. The number one offender for nonprofessional profile content is Facebook, so I recommend starting there.

Cleaning up your Facebook profile is not necessarily difficult; it can just be tedious depending on the volume of content and how non-PG rated the content is to start with. The major red flags you should be on the lookout for include humor in questionable taste, antagonistic interactions, and of course any "Gone Wild"-style photographs. Can you keep pictures up that show you holding a glass of wine? Absolutely. Should you keep a picture up that shows you after six glasses of wine? I would say no. Remember, the goal of rebranding your profile pages isn't to take away all their sense of personality or character but to frame them in a way that supports your larger career goals.

Since the concept of filtering Facebook content to meet acceptable standards for an employer or client can be hard to understand in abstract terms, I typically go by the following rule of thumb: if I wouldn't want my dad to see it, I shouldn't post it. Please feel free to use whichever family member, friend, or child makes the rule work for you.

# break it down: washing your face(book)

Here are some tips for getting your Facebook profile ready for professional use.

1. **Delete and untag.** Go through *all* the pictures that come up in the "photos" section of your profile—that includes the ones that you uploaded, your profile picture, and photos that others have tagged you in—and use your professional standards rule of thumb to weed out any that are questionable (or flat-out inappropriate).

   To do either of these functions, just look to the bottom-right of the pop-up window that showcases the full-sized picture. There should be a list of actions you can take regarding the photo, including deleting it if you were the uploader, or clicking a link that says "report/remove tag" if someone else uploaded it. Removing the tag won't take the picture offline, but it will keep it from popping up should someone search for you.

2. **Filter your wall.** Again, another tedious but necessary cleansing job. Maybe you have some less-than-coherent status updates; maybe your friends posted comments or inside jokes that, again, you wouldn't want your professional audience seeing. Depending on how long you have had your account, it is probably not worth your time to go in with the aim of filtering every wall post ever made (although if you feel so inclined, be my guest). Going through material from the last two to six months should be sufficient to keep any dubious details out of the wrong hands.

   Removing a wall post is pretty easy: just hover your cursor over the top-right of the post area and click on the little icon that appears (depending on the kind of post, it might be shaped like a globe or just an *x*). At the bottom of the drop-down menu you should see the option to "Remove

Post . . . " Be sure to click the second "Remove Post" button that pops up in the prompt, and you should be all set.

3. **Review your profile content.** At the top of your profile, you should see a little link next to a pencil icon that allowed you to "Edit Your Profile." You would be surprised what random and unprofessional bits can be lurking in this seemingly tame area of your profile. For example, a lot of my girlfriends used to list themselves as married to their best female friend to display their BFF-ness: kind of endearing in college, but potentially misconstrued later on. Another field where you might find some colorful input is in the Activities and Interests section.

Twitter and LinkedIn, perhaps due to their limited and specific capacities, tend to present less of an issue when it comes to weeding out unprofessional content . . . unless you are one of those people who like to get into it with other people via Twitter. You don't see 140 characters as the right medium to have a war of words? Then you might be surprised at the kind of knock-down, drag-out interactions that have been tweeted, especially among celebrities. All I can say is that hurling pithy insults back and forth over which season of *The Simpsons* was the best or who should be the next president isn't a great indicator to your target market of your being able to play nice with others. The good news is that even though all tweets are now being archived by the Library of Congress, you can still delete tawdry tweets out of your Twitter feed so that no one will see them when accessing your profile page. Again, as with your Facebook tidying, being sure the last two to six months of tweets are target-market-friendly is all you should concern yourself with, unless you know off the top of your head that something jaw-dropping lurks beyond the six-month mark.

Once your pages are tidied up, you can start officially rebranding them with the aim of communicating and promoting your APB to a whole new global network of connections. Several basic, must-have branding elements are applicable across all three sites. Let's take a look at these first, and then we'll look at individual suggestions for each platform.

### Use the Same Name

When I search for my friend Robert's profile on a social media site, it is always hit or miss as to whether I'll find it. Sometimes he's created a profile under "Robert," but sometimes he uses "Bob" or "Bobby." As if guessing which form of his first name he will use isn't annoying enough, sometimes he chooses to include his middle name, or just his middle initial. The result is that finding him online is usually a miss. For personal connections like this, I'll persevere until I find my friend. Do you think his target market, which in this case are potential clients, would be so patient? I think not.

When rebranding yourself across your social media pages, please do everyone including yourself a huge favor and use the exact same version of your name everywhere. Not only does this consistency make it easier to find you; it also supports the recognition of your professional brand.

### Use the Same Profile Picture

In many ways, your profile picture is like your online brand logo. This again speaks to the point about brand recognition, especially if there are a few other people out there with the same name as yours. I am lucky there aren't any other Nacie Carsons around, but I still use the same profile picture on all sites to support the quick recognition of my brand. Apple doesn't have a different logo for each of its social media profiles, and neither should you.

Be sure to choose a well-focused headshot. If you don't have any professional headshots, no worries—you likely have software on your computer right now that can crop a headshot from an existing picture. Just be careful about two things: your attire in the picture, and the background in the picture. Make sure your attire is age and industry appropriate. As far as the background goes, ask yourself if you'd be willing to include this picture with your next job application.

## Use Your Tagline and Your Story

Remember the tagline and the draft of your two-minute elevator speech that you crafted in Chapter Three? You are going to draw from that thought process when filling in the bio section of your social media profiles. Instead of simply listing your job title or the functions you perform, you should use the bio section of these websites to round out your identity as a multi-faceted individual in the mind of your target market. Use your tagline on Twitter, where you are allowed only 160 characters for your bio—that means essentially one carefully worded sentence. On Facebook, you can employ the two-minute version of your story. Facebook doesn't have a restriction on the length of your "About Me" section, but I have found the shorter you can be, the better. In spite of its short length (which could come across as a little abrupt), my tagline appears at the top of my Facebook bio; this supports continuity and brand recognition across both sites.

The fifteen-minute version of your professional story is best suited for the Summary section on LinkedIn. My summary on LinkedIn spans four paragraphs and touches on my APB offering and mission components. I use the same summary for the bio section on my website and send it as part of my materials for a speaking engagement.

Once you have these essential branding elements consistent across the three major platforms, you can start to tailor the communication of your APB to each of the platforms on the basis of their specific capabilities and tones.

## break it down: platform-specific rebranding tips

### To Rebrand Your Facebook Page:

**Fill out the entire profile.** Facebook breaks down your profile into eight categories: Basic Information, Friends and Family, Education and Work, Philosophy, Arts and Entertainment, Sports, Activities and Interests, and Contact Information. To get the most lift out of your presence on the site, I recommend filling in as much of this information as possible. The best way to use Facebook is as a personal-network development tool. People will connect better with you when they can learn something about you beyond your offering components. However, there are a few areas where discretion is advisable, like the religious affiliation and political views fields. Unless you consider either of these points to be a vital part of your APB or important to your target market, leave them blank. And take caution when sharing any personal contact information, such as your address or even your phone number. Common sense about internet safety should never be overridden for the sake of promoting your brand.

**Upload pictures.** As long as they are appropriate, a set of pictures on your Facebook page is a great way to deepen your ability to connect with others and to shape the physical presentation component of your APB. And don't think all the pictures need to be serious or business-oriented: photos of you picking apples with your friends, shoveling your car out of the snow, or playing with your dog are excellent ways to communicate your story and challenge that descriptor-box mentality. Photos are also great conversation starters, so they can help promote interactions on your profile. The same caution about internet safety applies: be careful not to post any pictures that show the license plate of your car, your street address, or any other identifying details.

### To Rebrand Your Twitter Presence:

**Pay attention to the background image.** When someone views your Twitter feed, the container that actually includes your tweets, bio, and other details takes up only the middle of the page. Depending on the size of the monitor someone is viewing the page on, there can be quite a bit of space on the left and right sides of your profile, which is filled with a background image. You can (and should) adjust the background image by going into your profile settings and choosing one of the prepackaged options under the "Design" tab. However, I recommend hiring a web designer if possible to build a personalized background so that you can leverage that space for your APB.

If you visit my Twitter page (http://www.twitter.com/Nacie Carson), you'll see a standard example of what you can achieve in this extra bit of space. I've had my web designer set up the background so that my e-mail, website information, Facebook page information, and website logo appear in the unused space on the left side of the Twitter feed container. Using this extra space for contact details frees up space (characters) in my bio field to share more of my story. I've seen people use this space for more about the mission component of their APB, more specific offering information in bullet points, or a collage of pictures that highlight their physical presentation. The cost of hiring a web designer to do this work can range from $100 to $400 depending on the designer's experience and how fancy you want to make the space, but I have found it to be worth every penny.

**Set up notifications.** Under your Twitter profile settings is a tab called "Notifications" that allows you to be e-mailed when some type of activity occurs on your Twitter feed, such as when someone replies to your tweet, you are sent a private message, or someone new subscribes to your feed. If you are new to Twitter, I highly recommend that you set up some of these notifications to get you in the habit of interacting on the site. The problem with all social media sites is that they are so easy to simply set up and then forget about. While that doesn't make them entirely useless for our purposes (you are still projecting your brand to potentially thousands of connections), it definitely leaves some leveraging chips on the table. You can turn notifications off easily once you get more accustomed to logging in and participating, but in the beginning it is a huge help.

### To Rebrand On Linkedin:

**Fill out the entire profile.** Just like Facebook, LinkedIn provides a whole set of profile input options to help you produce a robust profile. However, unlike Facebook, these are almost entirely career focused. Main fields include details about your current and past employment and positions, education (all the way back to grade school!), skill specialties (after the preceding chapter you should be all set on what to enter here), professional awards and honors, and any professional associations you belong to. One of the neatest features of the LinkedIn profile is the contact preferences list, where you can select what kinds of things people on the site can contact you about, from career opportunities to business ventures to expertise requests.

There are really no fields in the LinkedIn profile that I would caution you about, except for the standing caution about address and contact information. LinkedIn is such a great resource for projecting the offering component of your APB that it would be silly not to take advantage of it. Feeling lost about where to start? The site has a profile wizard that guides you through the process and tells you what's missing.

**Join groups.** On the navigation bar located at the top of your profile, you'll notice a tab named "Groups." Groups are exactly what they sound like: a collection of members coming together to interact around specific topics. There are groups for everything imaginable, from all kinds of professional organizations to college alumni to charitable efforts. I recommend that you sign up with a few groups for two reasons: (1) groups can help connect you with others and provide a good forum for interaction; and (2) when someone views your profile, a list of all the groups you belong to is visible, providing more detail on who you are as a professional.

**Solicit recommendations.** After you make some initial connections, use the Recommendations feature (located in the drop-down menu under "Profile") to solicit endorsements from people you have gone to school with, worked with, or provided a service to. The recommendations feature is one of the major selling points of LinkedIn as a place to not only project your APB but have others validate and support it. You can never have too many recommendations on your page, so keep soliciting them over time.

## making the most of your digital presentation

Once you have rebranded and set up your profile pages to successfully promote your APB, it's time to leverage them. Unfortunately, just setting up the pages isn't enough to experience their benefits. As Crystal notes, "If you build it, they won't come. You need to engage individuals, regularly, in order to build up your audience. This can be done in as little as ten to fifteen minutes a day, but it needs to be ongoing over time."

## quick tips for hiring a web designer

If you decide to take the route of hiring a professional web designer to create a personalized background for you, it is important to look for certain credibility indicators before allowing someone access to your profile or finances. The internet is full of people who are looking for uninformed individuals to prey on, and you don't want to be the prey. If you can't get a referral for a web designer (my preferred method of introduction), post an ad under the "gig" section of Craigslist and screen the respondents using the following tips:

- Visit their website to confirm they are legitimate
- Ask for testimonials from clients if none appear on the website
- Request live samples of their recent work
- Ask them to provide a mock-up of a background to see how they interpret your requests and to make sure you can effectively communicate with each other
- Before signing any contract, request a phone call to learn more about them in an interview format
- Ask them to send a copy of the contract and terms over for you to review prior to verbal (or written) agreement of their services

The number one challenge that is universal to the experience of social media is maintaining the right time-spent-to-rewards-gained ratio. On the one hand, it can be very easy to overengage online and waste time participating in interactions that feel helpful but are just time sucks. With so many people to interact with—many of them interesting, funny, or so awful they are entertaining—hours can slip away before your realize you didn't do half the truly productive things you needed to do. Think I am exaggerating? Consider this: researchers at Ohio State University have discovered that too much time on Facebook can cause a student's GPA to drop significantly.[8] Imagine what it can do to all of us adults in the "real world" who have financial responsibilities and a recession to overcome.

On the other hand, too little engagement on these sites can defeat a major purpose of having them: to actively network and promote your APB. Yet when you barely have enough time in the day to see your significant other, the idea of plopping down in front of your Twitter feed for a spell doesn't rank high on the list of priorities. So how do you strike the right balance? You schedule time to engage online like you would any other appointment. Crystal found that twenty minutes a day to interact online has been sufficient for her to see results. Personally, I try to take forty-five minutes in the morning while I am having my coffee to do my social media work for the day.

Aside from scheduling, many people find tools like Tweet-Deck helpful in managing all their social media profiles and conversations from one command center. TweetDeck is free, easily set up, and intuitive to use. Check it out at tweetdeck. com to learn more.

So you have the profiles set up and time carved out to use the sites. What do you do now?

The first thing you should do is build out your contact lists on all the sites—search for friends and family on Facebook, find leaders in your industry or your favorite authors (like me!) on Twitter, and connect with as many people from your professional past as possible on LinkedIn. The more people you can add to your social networks, the more people who will be exposed to your brand. Also, the greater chance you'll have of getting your APB communicated beyond your networks: when people repost, share, or retweet your interactions online, then all of their network sees it, bringing your name and brand to people you don't even know . . . yet!

As far as the interactions themselves go, I've discovered a few best practices for communicating on these sites:

- *Be authentic in your communications.* Whether you are sharing a career update on LinkedIn or responding to an industry leader on Twitter, always be yourself. If you are a little sarcastic in person, be a little sarcastic online. If you are supportive and gushing offline, let that come out in your communication. People can always smell a phony, even through cyberspace. You will make better connections with people when you are coming from a genuine place.

- *Share what interests you.* People log onto these sites to make connections and in an odd way be stimulated and entertained through the sharing of knowledge. If updating people about the comings and goings of your life, profes-sional or otherwise, feels too intimate for you, try encour-aging people to check out things that you find interesting. News articles, books, music are all fair game.

- *Provide expertise.* A great way to build a reputation for yourself as an expert in a particular area or skill set is to focus your updates around that topic. You can provide people in your social network industry advice or how-to tips to earn a digital name for yourself in one of the skill areas we outlined in the last chapter. However, be careful not to provide too much unsolicited advice, or advice that sounds self-righteous—neither will go over well!

- *Ask questions of your network.* A great way to balance out giving too much advice is to solicit advice yourself from your social networks. You can ask questions about business topics or use questions as a great way to show a little personality without making it a central theme of your online presence. Posting a question to your network is a fine way to start a dialogue and allow other people to bring their brands to your profile.

- *Consider quality over quantity.* Unless you are in the feline products or breeding industry, writing ninety-nine tweets about your cat, Mr. Wellington, won't advance your brand much. Quality over quantity wins every time, even in the social media space. If you are in doubt about whether to post something, just ask yourself if you think someone else would find it valuable or interesting.

- *Share other people's updates.* A great way to build goodwill and connections via social media is to highlight what other people are doing by reposting it, sharing it, or retweeting it through your profile. "Liking" something on Facebook also accomplishes the same goal.

- *Always keep your target market in mind.* As you get comfortable in the social media space with your APB, remember that your goal is to connect and develop relationships with your target market. In all the goings-on across social media, it can be easy to lose sight of the needs and messages for this audience.

Above all, as you use social media to build out and leverage your adaptive professional brand, remember that at their core, Facebook, Twitter, and LinkedIn are just digital spaces designed to promote conversation. The same basic rules that govern successful in-person interactions apply here as well: try to be interested, not interesting; it's not polite to monopolize conversation; and people don't want to hear all about you all the time.

These sites are not the only conversation forums for your career, but in our rapidly globalizing and internet-connected world, they are gaining in importance every day. And for us members of the Fittest who have taken ownership of our professional futures and brands, they can provide an invaluable network of opportunity, clientele, and support. This is especially the case when we decide to utilize the final strategy of the Finch Effect: *Harness your entrepreneurial energy.*

# 6

# harness your
# entrepreneurial energy

With the first strategy of the Finch Effect, you adopted a gig mindset and reclaimed ownership of and power over your career. Now, in the fifth and final strategy of the Finch Effect, you will harness that sense of individual ownership by incorporating entrepreneurial tactics and methods into your career strategy. In other words, you'll find ways to think and act strategically, like an entrepreneur and owner of your own career path, no matter what your employment circumstances are.

It's interesting the way people react to the word "entrepreneur." They seem to use a kind of absolute logic that makes them either completely identify with the term or completely separate themselves from it. It's the same sort of thought process that people approach creativity with—to my mind, the statements "I am not creative" and "I am not entrepreneurial" have a lot in common. Yet we all have entrepreneurial potential. Members of the Fittest know it and act accordingly. Entrepreneurial capability is a basic human attribute, and we live in a time when it's possible—and a smart idea—to develop that potential.

How does the concept of being entrepreneurial resonate with you? If you don't identify with it, I encourage you to re-evaluate your understanding of the term. In a great opinion piece for the *Washington Post*, Vivek Wadhwa, the director of research at the Center for Entrepreneurship and Research Commercialization at Duke University, enumerated the top commonly held misconceptions about typical American entrepreneurship. He noted that the stereotypes we see in the news, like Mark Zuckerberg and Bill Gates, paint a picture for the rest of us that in order to be a successful entrepreneur, you need to be a technology visionary, a genius 20-something, or a college dropout with a healthy disdain for being a sheep in the system (and it helps to have a gift for winning over venture capitalists with your nonconformist visions and uncompromising attitude).[1]

But the truth is that entrepreneurs in this country come from all backgrounds, industries, and base funding amounts. Their business endeavors can grow into small or midsized businesses, or can remain one-man shops. From what I've observed about members of the Fittest and learned from my own experience, age, education, and industry have nothing to do with an individual's potential to be an entrepreneur. The only requirements are a desire to create vocational opportunity for yourself and the initiative, direction, and sense of ownership to do so. Simply put, an entrepreneur is someone who is enterprising.

Part of being a member of the Fittest is embodying this kind of entrepreneurship—whether you are creating a new business or just a new opportunity within your current career. The Fittest understand that other people may present you with opportunities but that often, in order to best advance your career and support your adaptive professional brand, you need to create them yourself.

I am not going to spend the rest of the chapter trying to talk you into going professionally rogue (although we will go there for a while). But I am going to try to talk you into harnessing what I call *entrepreneurial energy* to support your career success as a member of the Fittest.

The simplest explanation of entrepreneurial energy comes down to the practical application of the gig mindset you have cultivated in the first Finch Effect strategy. The entire premise of the first strategy is that once you make the mental shift to owning your career, and adjust your perspective to ownership, you will be in a position to take action and succeed regardless of what is going on in the job market. Entrepreneurial energy fuels that action, and it can be utilized in several ways.

One way members of the Fittest use entrepreneurial energy is by approaching their work as employees in a way that further differentiates them from their peers and increases their value to the organization. As I've mentioned before, some of the skills and business tactics that have served me best as an employee are ones I learned when working for myself.

Another way that the Fittest expend entrepreneurial energy is by diversifying their income sources through business endeavors outside their current job. Working on the side can help you build expertise in your industry, thus making you more valuable as an employee. If you lose your job or find your

hours reduced, having established work outside of your traditional job can serve not only as a means of monetary support
but also as a launchpad for the next step in your career.

A final Fittest way to harness entrepreneurial energy is to
actually jump the employer ship and become a full-fledged
entrepreneur. Depending on where you are in your career,
what your lifestyle needs are, and what's going on in your industry, striking out on your own may be the best way to adapt
and succeed in the job market.

In this chapter, we will examine each of these three uses of
entrepreneurial energy in depth to discover which application
is the right fit for your current situation and adaptive professional brand. As we explore each more deeply, I encourage you
to keep your mind open and alert, even if you think you know
which tactic you will pursue. We know by now that the key
to our vocational success is an ever evolving refinement of
our Finch Effect skills as our needs and the needs of the job
market change.

So let's go once more unto the breach, dear friends, and get
to work on harnessing your entrepreneurial energy.

## entrepreneurial energy and the f-word

Can you think of a time when you failed? I mean really failed?

I can, several times, and they are all embarrassing to think
about. It's amazing how an experience of totally dropping the
ball can make you sensitive to the possibility of future failure.
In fact, the most frightening element of entrepreneurship is
the real possibility of failure. Even when we ask ourselves the
"right" questions about the risks and rewards of starting our
own venture, there is no escaping the fact that failure is a

potential outcome. And in a dicey economy, it is normal that the fear of failure is more acute than it might be in better job markets.

As we begin to examine the benefits and limitations of harnessing your entrepreneurial energy to thrive as a member of the Fittest, I'd like you to acknowledge the presence of the "f-word" in your mind and think about what would happen in the event that you did fail professionally. Self-limiting beliefs about failure, much like the concept of confirmation bias we talked about in the second chapter, have the capacity to poison our perspective, drawing it away from seeing and seizing on information and opportunities to use our entrepreneurial energy and thrive.

Let's break down what would happen if you actually and truly failed.

First, you'd probably be embarrassed or angry. I can tell you that when I fail I feel keenly the stupidity, injustice, and unfairness of it all. If you ever need help becoming aware of your negative self-talk, all you have to do is fail, and you will hear it inescapably loud and clear.

Then, depending on the nature of the failure, there might be some consequences, like lost members of your target market, wasted money, or a damaged reputation. And then there might be some penance, like slaps on the wrist from superiors, the slow rebuilding of broken trust, or the even slower refilling of the piggy bank. And then what?

Nothing. That's about all failure is made of.

Some failures might take longer than others to recover from, but typically, failures—even epic ones—are pretty short-lived affairs. Think about celebrity scandals, even the worst one you can imagine: they are all anyone can talk about for about a week, and then suddenly they're off the world's radar. Our failures, though they're less public, have about the same half-life, for one simple reason: contrary to our pervasive belief (and we all share this one), the rest of the world isn't thinking about or paying attention to us all the time. A good scandal is compelling enough to pull people out of their self-centric, internal dialogues for a short burst of time, but sooner rather than later we all want to get back to thinking about ourselves and our own issues, not others'.

The truth is that what makes a failure persist is our inability to let it go. Our emotional bruises from failure have a way of shutting us down and preventing us from learning and growing from it. We adopt failure as part of our perspective, and begin to perceive our situation and place in the world through the context of those experiences. It can be a really limiting way to live and work. The worst thing about having such a perspective is that it can be self-fulfilling. It's not surprising then that we are less likely to be defined by our successes than by the way we embrace our failures.

Actually, failures can open up golden opportunities to succeed if you know how to handle them. Hardly any successful people have never experienced significant failure—and the most spectacularly successful people have likely experienced spectacular failure at some point. And have grown from it.

In my understanding, there are four main approaches people take to turning entrepreneurial failure into success: persistence, alternating the venue, reworking strategies, and starting over.

The *persistence* method is short and simple: if at first you don't succeed, try, try again until you do. The persistence method works when you believe that what you are doing is right and that eventually it will yield the result you want. If you know you have a good idea, you don't stop until it works. Tenacity and not taking no for an answer (even if you actually *get* no for an answer over and over) can sometimes be the best way to push through the wall of failure and reach success on the other side. For example, you open a business in a location that might not be yielding immediate returns, but you believe it will be a prime location in a matter of time as a result of other community development.

Yet sometimes it's not the idea that is failing; it is *where* you are implementing it. The *alternating the venue* method for turning failure into success works by moving a sound strategy to a different venue for implementation. If your business is not doing well at the initial location, you decide to relocate to another part of town where more of your target audience can be found, or you take it online and ditch the brick-and-mortar shop.

The method of *reworking strategies* is characterized by examining your whole approach, cutting out parts that are not helping, and implementing new strategies. To continue our example, you decide not only to change the location of the store but also to adjust its layout, redesign your logo, and streamline your product offerings to increase their customer appeal.

This method requires a willingness to pull your goal strategy apart, analyze what's working and what isn't, and then put it back together . . . maybe with parts from another strategy patched in here and there. This is more time consuming than the first two methods as it constitutes a partial return to the drawing board. It's a good approach to take when you know your strategy needs reevaluating but there are salvageable elements.

A fourth approach to turning failure into success is the aptly named *starting over* method. This we do when the whole enterprise has failed. We take our dreams back to the drawing board and start from scratch. Sometimes our plans for success seem like great ideas at the time, and only failure exposes the holes in our strategies, showing us how to correct course and start anew. This might mean closing the store altogether, cutting our losses, and reexamining the product concept entirely. To take this approach, we have to be willing to look at our failure squarely and analyze it carefully, not flinch away from it in shame and disappointment.

And that can be hard to do.

In fact, many people see this final method as the embodiment of failure: you tried, it didn't work, and now you have to start over with nothing to show for it. This is not true, of course. What you have to show for the first attempt is wisdom, experience, and an idea of what *not* to do. How many ways did they say Thomas Edison found to not make a light bulb? It was a lot, but the exact number doesn't matter, just the idea. When you fail and have to start over, you have just found a way to avoid not getting what you want.

You have to admit, when you look past the stigma of failing, there is something liberating about using the starting-over method. As far as I am concerned, the only true failure is allowing yourself to accept failure. Trying, failing, and succeeding are all parts of our evolution and growth. We shouldn't be afraid of embracing our entrepreneurial energy, one of our most powerful capabilities as members of the Fittest, for fear of failure. With so many ways to handle any failure that comes our way, entrepreneurial or otherwise, we have no reason not to jump at the chance to wield that energy and use it to thrive.

## using entrepreneurial energy
## inside your organization

What does it mean to "use entrepreneurial energy inside your organization"? Simply put, it means thinking like an entrepreneur while acting like an employee.

Traditionally, the roles of employee and entrepreneur represent two completely different professional archetypes, each with their own ideal skill set. For example, success for employees is often measured by how well they take direction from superiors, act within the scope of their job responsibilities or functions, and reinforce the mission, vision, or values of the organization. Success for entrepreneurs is typically determined by their ability to direct their own work and act without precedent, to expand and grow their job responsibilities and functions, and to envision and support a mission, vision, and set of values on their own. Another way to look at it is to think of the role of the employee as implementing the *tactics* of an organization—the individual actions that contribute to the success of the larger strategy. The role of entrepreneurs is to develop that larger *strategy* and implement it themselves or oversee its implementation.

From my experience in professional development and management consulting, I can tell you that the number one complaint organizations have about their employees is their inability to act tactically but think strategically—or, as above, to act like an employee but think like an entrepreneur. This requires being a follower and a leader simultaneously, and knowing which hat to wear when. Understandably, employees who can pull off this nuanced balancing act are a rarity—to the consternation of organizations that need this combination of tactical action and strategic thought to keep innovating, setting new standards, and adapting themselves to economic conditions. The result is that employees who can meet the requirements of their job while also contributing to and improving the strategic leadership of their organization are worth their weight in gold to their employers.

Steve can tell you firsthand. While working as a software analyst for a major financial firm, he was given the responsibility of managing a large collection of computer scripts that were integral to accurately processing the firm's data. The opportunity was a big one, especially for a member of the team who had been with the firm for just a year after college. The only problem was that the computer scripts had been originally written at an amateur level. Data that influenced forecasting models were delayed daily, jeopardizing informed investment decisions. Steve was in a tough position, "I hadn't written any of this code, but that didn't stop anyone from blaming me for the daily data problems. I owned the code, after all."

After a month of trying to manage the subpar code, he realized he needed to approach the issue from a more entrepreneurial angle. Acting without precedent, Steve started "pouring effort" into rebuilding the code from scratch using the latest coding language. "I didn't ask permission," he notes. "I saw what needed to be done and I did it. In the end my solution might have been rejected by management. Months of work would have been cast aside. I would have been disappointed, but I also would have tried again."

But starting over wasn't necessary, as his solution effectively solved the problem. "After a month I had rebuilt most of the scripts, and within two months I had totally redesigned the data processing system. What used to break every day and take hours to fix now broke once a week or less and could usually be fixed in a few minutes. Daily data was now available before most analysts had even pulled into the parking lot and, more importantly, it was far more accurate."

The entrepreneurial energy Steve harnessed to take ownership and solve a big issue in his organization yielded tangible dividends as well: he was promoted twice in his first year on the job and received an off-cycle bonus to reward his efforts. I'll say it again: employees who can meet the requirements of their job while also contributing to and improving the strategic leadership of their organization are worth their weight in gold to their employers. As Steve's experience shows, members of the Fittest who want to remain in their current organizations have found that harnessing their entrepreneurial energy to help meet their role requirements has led to improved performance, differentiation from their peers, and an overall increase in their professional worth.

Additionally, people who are interested in staying in their industry but shifting organizations have found the use of their entrepreneurial energy helpful for developing and communicating their APB to their target market. In spite of the positive reputation Steve had cultivated at his firm, in large part due to his ability to think like an entrepreneur but act like an employee, he decided to leave after two years to go work at a start-up. The projects he had used his entrepreneurial energy to drive at his previous firm were excellent vehicles for sharing his APB with his new company, InsightSquared. But six months later, he was getting calls from his old managers at the large financial firm asking him to come back. "They had designed a position specifically for me and were offering me a much better salary than I had been making when I left. But the start-up was a better overall fit. I've already made the leap from 40,000th employee to 6th employee, and after this it might be time to find out what it's like to be the 1st employee."

I learned a host of entrepreneurial skills after I left my nine-to-five to build my writing career in 2008—skills like market research and business management, which had been foreign to me as an employee. But when I found myself working again as an employee several years later, I was able to harness those entrepreneurial skills to my advantage, and my organization's. The most important of these has been productivity. Not only did I find my productivity skills easily transferred from entrepreneurial endeavors to an employee situation, but I also found they did more to enhance my professional worth than the other skills I had learned.

When you're a writer, productivity can sometimes feel subjective: "Oh, I didn't get that much down on paper today, but I did a lot of 'mental work' on my article/blog/book." Yeah, that was an excuse I found myself making in the early freelancing days. What I soon realized was that "mental work" days were all well and good . . . until I was scrambling to pay my electric bill.

When your livelihood depends on self-imposed productivity, you either get good at it or you find yourself in mounds of debt. The initial bloom of freedom that came from not needing to be chained to a desk for a set of specific hours every day withered a little when I discovered that I had no idea how to get things done unless I had a boss to answer to. Productivity—real, self-driven productivity—was one of the first entrepreneurial skills I learned. It served me well when I was on my own, and it has served me even better as an employee because it requires a kind of organization and self-motivation that employees aren't necessarily incentivized to cultivate. After all, if you are super-productive, all you'll get is more work to do, right?

Yes, and in more than one sense. You may be assigned more responsibilities and tasks, but you will also likely be offered more opportunity in the organization . . . as long as you make sure someone notices the effort. Like the proverbial tree falling in the forest, if a man works eighty hours a week and no one sees him, does he still get a raise? (No.) This is why productivity, when combined with a great adaptive professional brand, is an awesome recipe for increasing your value within an organization.

## break it down: build your productivity skills

Here are a few productivity lessons that transfer well between entrepreneurial ventures and employee situations:

**Allow yourself to procrastinate**. If you find yourself sitting at your desk and staring into space or surfing through articles on Cracked.com for a few hours, then you are likely procrastinating. Procrastination often corresponds to certain parts of the day (3 P.M., anyone?) or is linked to fatigue and burnout. When you are being unproductive and avoidant of your job tasks, then it is probably in your best interest to get up and away from your workstation for a while (perhaps twenty to forty-five minutes). Walk around the office, talk to your coworkers, take a coffee break, and if possible get outside for some sunshine. Sitting at your station just because you think you have to is foolish and ineffective. If anyone says something to you about it, be honest: sometimes you just have to go where the procrastination takes you. Note: This strategy should be used with caution; it can easily turn into an excuse for inaction if used too often!

**Learn your attention schedule**. The problem I have always found with the nine-to-five model (aside from the fact that it's crumbling underneath us) is that it isn't conducive to our individual attention schedules. Not everyone is at his mental best from 9 A.M. to 5 P.M. exactly. Some may do better work in the morning; others, later in the day. Unless you have a boss who is open to flexible scheduling, you will need to pay attention to your own attention peaks and valleys during the day, and then try to build your daily tasks around them. For example, if you observe that you do your best work in the morning, try to keep your hours before lunch clear and schedule meetings and so forth in the afternoon.

**Replace to-dos with goals**. Supplement your to-do task list at work with a list of goals to be accomplished. In 1968, Edwin Locke, who studied the psychology of achievement and success, reported that employees who had clear goals achieved much more than those who had nebulous tasks or didn't understand the ultimate goal of their responsibilities.[2] When you see the larger picture of each task—the strategy—you are more motivated to complete it quickly and with higher quality, as opposed to just looking at a list of unrelated or uninspiring tasks.

Productivity is just one example of a traditional employee skill that I am able to leverage for my APB within my organization because I bring my entrepreneurial perspective to it. You can do this with other skills, even if you don't have an entrepreneurial background, by conducting a thought experiment. What would you need to do to maintain or increase your success with that skill if you became the CEO tomorrow? Or better yet, imagine that all of your higher-ups were on vacation for a few years and you needed to accomplish your workload without any direction or anyone checking up on you. What would you do? The point is to look at your job responsibilities and required skills from a place of ownership, initiative, and personal direction. Remember, it's about tactics *and* strategy.

## break it down: should i stay or should i go?

A major misconception that arises in recessions or down economic times is that career mobility is on hold. Not so! Actually, if we have the intestinal fortitude to see it, a great benefit of an evolving job market is that all options need to be on the table. It may seem counterintuitive, but now is not the time to consent to staying at an organization that doesn't meet your strategic needs or support your APB.

This exercise asks you to reflect on and move past your perceptions on job mobility in a recession, and provide an authentic and comprehensive answer to the question "Should I stay in my job or move on?"

To begin, try to relax and focus your thoughts on the exercise. Allow yourself about a half hour of undisrupted time to consider the following questions. I encourage you to write your answers to each on a separate piece of paper—this will help you organize your thoughts and also give you space to write down further thoughts that develop and be as specific as possible.

- What do you like about your current job? Please list everything and then visualize each item on the list.
- What don't you like about your current job? Please list everything and then visualize each item on the list.
- What about your company's mission, vision, or values resonates with you? Please list everything and then visualize each item on the list.
- What about your company makes you frustrated? Please list everything and then visualize each item on the list.

- Can you describe a typical "good" day at work for you? Please be as detailed as possible.
- Can you describe a typical "bad" day at work for you? Please be as detailed as possible.
- Can you describe a time in the past six months at your job where you felt in control of your career or felt satisfied? Please be as detailed as possible.
- Can you describe a time in the past six months at your job when you felt out of control of your career or distressed? Please be as detailed as possible.

This exercise is extremely valuable, not only for gauging whether you want to stay in your particular job but for assessing how you can more effectively channel your entrepreneurial energy. If you like your organization, you can use your entrepreneurial energy to cultivate new opportunities for yourself through using that energy inside your organization. If you want to explore other options within your field or start to branch out in a new field altogether, you will find harnessing your energy outside of your organization to be most useful. Let's take a look at what that means.

## using entrepreneurial energy outside your organization

If you are concerned about the stability of your industry or organization, or if you want to continue to develop your adaptive professional brand beyond the scope of your company, then you should consider harnessing your entrepreneurial energy outside of your organization.

Adding some on-the-side entrepreneurial endeavors may seem like just one more thing to fit into your already strapped schedule, but the benefits can make it well worthwhile. What benefits, you may ask? How about:

- Potential for additional income: picking up a few gigs outside of work can put extra money in your pocket for savings, debt reduction, or a monthly manicure
- Experience as a consultant, freelancer, or entrepreneur: self-directed career experience communicates to people reading your résumé that you are motivated and capable of independent work
- Diversified source of revenue and job opportunities (all eggs *not* in one basket): should anything in your current career situation change suddenly for the worse, the extra income you receive from clients can help soften the blow and get you back on your feet faster
- Networking and additional APB promotion opportunities: working as a service provider can help you line up the next big career move without even applying for a job
- Practice, should you want to take the on-the-side work full-time: managing your client work while you still have the safety of another job reduces the risk of entrepreneurship and allows you to learn on the job without worrying as much about the consequences of failure
- Building your expertise and gaining more experience in your field; exposure to more experience while still employed at another organization: if you are a young professional, this is an especially good way to build out your résumé quickly

An additional benefit to using your entrepreneurial energy outside of your organization is the capacity to further specialize your skill set and continue to stand out from the crowd by creating a professional niche. By focusing your on-the-side work on something related to but tangential to your job or industry, you are adding another unique skill combination to the offering component of your professional brand. You will also likely be chasing a slightly different target market than your peers. If you are a sales consultant with a CPA or a doctor with an MBA, what positions or opportunities might you qualify for that you wouldn't if you were just a sales consultant or a doctor?

You have heard the phrase "a big fish in a small pond," referring to being the best in a small pool of competitors. When I say create and fill your own niche, I don't mean be a big fish in a small pond; I mean be the only fish in a pond of your making. All you need is a little imagination and a fresh perspective on your current career to identify how your entrepreneurial energy can do just that.

## using entrepreneurial energy while unemployed

Job seekers who are underemployed or unemployed or even soon-to-be graduates can use this "outside your organization" entrepreneurial energy to balance part-time work (or job hunting) with building out their APBs. The first thing I thought of when I spoke to Kathleen on the phone in October 2009 was, "This woman could sell ketchup on a stick." Her voice, both authoritative and cool, and her eloquent manner of speaking made it immediately apparent that she was perfectly suited to her field: public relations.

Just one month earlier, Kathleen had been laid off from her position as public relations director at an electric cooperative in

Fort Meyers, Florida. "They told me it was my last day about fifteen minutes after I walked into the office," she sighed. "I really thought I was going to be there for many more years."

Kathleen knew she wanted to stay in her field and couldn't wait to get back into the action. After a week of feeling bummed that her friends were at work while she was home alone, she had an epiphany: "Just because I am unemployed doesn't mean I have to put my career on hold." So instead of focusing only on a job search, she kept equal focus on ways to advance her career in spite of the fact that she was unemployed. And so Kathleen Taylor, member of the Fittest, was born.

One of her main strategies was to seek out freelance PR opportunities to bring in some cash and add jobs and references to her résumé. To do this, she worked her network: "I am president of my local chapter of the Florida Public Relations Association, so I made sure I told my board and other members of my professional network that I was available for freelance projects. A lot of them had some contracted work offers they were able to toss my way, helping me to stay afloat and take the reins of my career."

Now, instead of debating how to proceed, Kathleen is embracing the ability to expand her industry experience while she continues to develop her next career move. "Who knows what fantastic opportunity is waiting for me next? I am watching, waiting, and preparing. And in the meantime, I am taking one of the first breaks of my adult life to . . . well . . . breathe."

Kathleen's robust embrace of freelancing, even as she stays alert to the next right thing, is a great example of on-the-side use of entrepreneurial energy. Here are a few concrete suggestions for exercising your entrepreneurial capacity to build your brand whether you are happily employed at the moment or not:

- Publish industry-related material in relevant digital and print presentation; most journals share their submission policies on their websites
- Provide consulting for people outside your industry: offer to provide your specific service to a neighbor, friend, or relative
- Build a website and deliver specialized content to fill a need in your industry
- Prepare and deliver your own portfolio showcase: for example, find spaces to hang your own photographs, or display information on real estate you are currently representing
- Set up or join a start-up nonprofit and use your expertise to advance its mission

When it comes to harnessing your entrepreneurial energy outside your organization, doing it for free—as unappealing as that may sound—isn't a bad strategy. Roberta Chinsky Matuson, blogger for Fast Company online and president of Human Resource Solutions, notes, "When doing this, be sure to establish clear guidelines. . . . For example, rather than tying yourself up five days a week, offer to [provide your service] two days a week. Be sure you have settled on a role that will enhance your skills. If all you are going to be doing is fetching coffee, then you might as well apply for a paid job at a coffee shop."[3]

Or if you have the desire, you could just start your own coffee shop . . .

## using entrepreneurial energy to build your organization

In the fall of 2009, I had the opportunity to chat with Howard Stephen Berg, master entrepreneur and the Guinness World Record holder for speed-reading. Formerly a New York City public school teacher, Berg won his title in 1990 for his ability to read 25,000 words per minute, and since then has parlayed that talent into a multimillion dollar business, authoring seven books and developing the Mega Speed Reading program, which has grossed over $65 million since its launch. In the summer of 2009, he starred in an endorsement for the Sony eReader alongside Justin Timberlake, who, Berg reported to me, is "a nice young man and great entrepreneur" (to my *NSYNC heart's disappointment, Berg remained professional and refused to give me his contact info).

Berg is a perennial champion for entrepreneurialism. "Why are people even looking for jobs?" he blustered in his New York accent. "We live in a capitalist country. Go out and build a company!" Now a grandfather, Berg is insistent that American workers—especially the younger generations—start thinking entrepreneurially to stay competitive with foreign competition: "Other countries are developing strong entrepreneurial mindsets and we need to keep pace in order to keep up with the world." In his mind, there are no better candidates for this responsibility than young professionals; he sees them as being more open to learning and adapting than older workers.[4]

While Berg was chatting with me about the glories of entrepreneurialism on the East Coast, three thousand miles away in Orange County, California, Christin was preparing to sit back down at her computer after a leisurely lunch.

Christin, 31, was laid off from her job as a digital music consultant in July 2008. As a consultant, Christin didn't qualify for unemployment benefits and needed a way to start bringing in money before she devoured her savings. "I became so desperate that I even applied for minimum-wage retail jobs. I didn't receive any callbacks on jobs I applied for, and in retrospect I think that was a blessing, because for the first time in my life I am truly passionate about what I do for a living."

After three months of trying to get back into the traditional workforce, Christin committed to getting herself back on track, just a completely different one. Instead of continuing to perceive her situation as something tragic, Christin shifted her thought process and started looking for a new opportunity. The result? "I finally took the leap and started my own business. I had been developing an idea for a business for about three years but didn't really have time to pursue it since I'd been working full time. I started Green 4 Your Soul, a one-stop shop for all things green. By June of 2009, I had launched my business website, and I continue to build my client base daily. I look forward to working every day, a feeling I never had while working corporate jobs."

Now, while most of her friends are still stuck in the daily grind, Christin is reveling in making her own schedule and running her own business. "I find that I work around the clock including weekends, but I try to mix things up so I don't get too burnt out or overwhelmed in one sitting. I never feel overworked like I did working in corporate America."

Her typical daily schedule is enough to make any full-time employee green with envy. Here is what a day in the life of Christin Sheehe, entrepreneur and member of the Fittest, looks like:

- Wake up around 7 A.M. and enjoy breakfast in my garden near the tranquil pond. I love sipping coffee while planning my day.
- Around 8 A.M. I respond to client inquiries and e-mails, and post updates on social networking sites.
- Around 10:30 A.M., after I've worked out and showered, I work on writing descriptions for new product lines and test products.
- Lunch happens sometime between 12 P.M. and 2 P.M., not really a set time. Just whenever I feel like it. When I am not out walking my dogs near the lake, I can be found reading on the patio, soaking up the rays of the sun, and enjoying the neighborhood . . .

It's incredible to think that just a year ago she was battling depression over being unemployed. What's even more incredible is that I have heard many similar stories from other members of the Fittest around the country who harnessed their entrepreneurial energy to successfully—and happily—strike out on their own: the advertising account manager turned self-employed photographer, the big-firm lawyer who opened her own specialized practice, or the insurance agent who now runs her own boutique jewelry store in her hometown. Taking the plunge into entrepreneurship is particularly attractive to professionals who have seen opportunities in their industry dry up over the last few years, getting outsourced to foreign labor markets or replaced with technological solutions. It is also attractive to those who are itching to break out of the nine-to-five routine and pursue their passions as their occupations.

At first blush, starting your own business in a down economy might seem like a bad idea. After all, if the huge corporate guys with hundreds of millions to play with are teetering on the brink of disaster, why would a microbusiness fare any better? In a September 2011 article in *USA Today*, Laura Petrecca notes that thought processes like this are causing the number of self-employed Americans (incorporated and unincorporated) to remain stagnant since the recession started in 2008. She lists financial concerns and a lack of confidence as the major reasons why people are backing away from entrepreneurial paths.[5]

And while Christin's patio-filled schedule does seem like a slice of heaven for those of us who are office bound, it's not all dog walking and sun-soaking. She acknowledges the inherent challenges of entrepreneurship along with the benefits: "You are going to have to work harder since you are not working for someone else, but if you are doing what you love it doesn't feel like work. Because twenty-four/seven you are getting the word out on your business. And if you do that, you can quickly build a following and a living."

In spite of reports noting a decrease in self-employed Americans, an August 2011 data report from the Bureau of Labor Statistics shows that there are still over fourteen million Americans who are self-employed, even in the face of double-dip recession woes. And when it comes to starting your own business, the news isn't all doom and gloom: commercial real estate is down, making office space more affordable to lease; thanks to the internet, setting up an effective online marketing campaign is fast and inexpensive; and with an almost double-digit unemployment rate, finding customers for a product or service may be no more difficult than finding a job. As far as the security piece goes, I beg to differ: with such high unemployment, it is hard for this observer of the Fittest to believe that a full-time job is any more of a sure thing than working for yourself.

But even with these motivating points, I can't tell you that there is no real risk to starting your own business. In any economy, good or bad, some ventures will succeed and some will fail. Others will plug along unspectacularly until the creator moves on to a new project or sells it to someone who can make it succeed. How yours would fare is a matter of a million factors, including preparation, determination, passion, and a healthy dose of luck.

## break it down: what's your entrepreneurial readiness?

If you are starting to consider the possibility that now or sometime down the road you might branch out on your own as an entrepreneur, here are some prompts to help you consider how ready you are, both mentally and logistically, to handle the risks and potential outcomes of entrepreneurship:

- Do you have any capital available to fund start-up costs? What kind of capital?
- Do you have enough savings set aside to buffer your personal expenses while the business is starting up (and do you have a realistic sense of how long that will take)?
- Do you consider yourself disciplined, self-motivated, and driven to succeed?
- Do you prefer taking direction or giving direction?

- Do you have any fitness, health, or lifestyle goals that would be supported, or undermined, by starting your own business?
- Can you work from home effectively, or do you need to have a separate office to work?
- Is a network of coworkers whom you see on a daily basis important to you?
- Are you prepared to take a cut in earnings as a potential tradeoff for a different lifestyle? How much do you need to live on, and how realistic is it that your venture would net this minimum within a reasonable time frame?
- If you're married or have a life partner, do you have their support? Do they share your ideas of the potential risks and rewards of entrepreneurship?
- If your entrepreneurial venture failed, how would you respond?
- Do you have a strong support system you can reach out to in times of need?

Take a minute to review your responses to these prompts. Do you see any trends or recurring themes that give you pause about pursuing an entrepreneurial endeavor? I have found that seeing your responses to these questions written out in your own hand can help you sort through your feelings and determine if this is the right way to move your career forward.

When you take an entrepreneurial leap, even your best-laid plans are subject to greater than normal instances of Murphy's Law; that is to say, if it can go wrong it will. So if you are planning to make the leap, you need to plan for extra resources to handle the inevitable arrival of unanticipated costs. Before you get started, it's not a bad idea to double or even triple what you think you might need to be on the safe side. Tony just opened his own pizza shop . . . six months later than expected. After leasing the commercial space in November 2010, he found himself trying to repair an obscure part of an old pizza oven and battling the local town board for the licenses they required. The store opened, and it's lovely—although it would have been lovelier if Tony hadn't blown all his savings on maintaining the rent, electricity, gas, water, and spoiled food costs for months before opening.

I share this story with you not to deter you from opening your own pizza place (I would never stand in the way of more pizza in the world!) but to remind you that when things go wrong—and they will—remember the mentality of ownership that you cultivated in Chapter Two. Successful entrepreneurship is about focusing on what you can problem-solve, doing your homework, and learning how to fail, successfully.

## break it down: blue-skying your entrepreneurial pursuit

The point of this exercise is to start brainstorming potential entrepreneurial pursuits, free from conceptual limitations about what is possible or sensible. I want you to consider and answer each of these questions as if there were no recession, and allow yourself to be as creative as you can be. Let your thoughts move organically. Don't think realistically—think potentially! The sky is the limit here, and your answers should reflect free and unbound thought. Allow yourself about fifteen minutes of quiet time to complete this exercise.

- If there were no chance for failure, what would you choose to do for a living?

- If you had an unlimited supply of money and time to pursue any dream, what would it be?
- If you didn't have to worry about financial security, what skills would you choose to learn? How about languages? Is there a particular thing you would like to become an expert on?
- If you could control what the world remembered you for, what would it be and how would you have done it?

## harnessing your entrepreneurial energy for good

The real value of harnessing your entrepreneurial energy is that it expands the ways in which you are capable of adapting to and thriving among changes in the job market. As culture and the economy continue to shift over the course of your career, you will almost certainly find that your success as a professional calls for using this energy in different ways: at some points you may need to run your own business venture, while at other times finding a way to leverage your entrepreneurial potential within an organization might serve you best.

One of the great tensions in the career-long journey of professional evolution is maintaining a balance between comfort and discomfort. We all have a vocational comfort zone: that role, set of responsibilities, or skill set that feels safe, familiar, and competent. Our natural instinct is to retreat into this comfort zone, especially during periods of high stress or major upset. But as members of the Fittest, we balance living in that comfort zone with embracing the discomfort associated with change, transition, and adaptation. If we err too far on the side of comfort, we miss the rewards and opportunities that can come from challenging ourselves and stretching our boundaries of resilience and potential. Yet if we err too far on the side of discomfort, we lose touch with the solid base that keeps our forward progress grounded and stable even amid the stress and anxiety of change.

The importance of this balance between comfort and discomfort is especially evident when you work to deploy your entrepreneurial energy in your career. As I noted earlier in the chapter, many people perceive a lot of stress and anxiety around entrepreneurship, especially in its full-fledged form. While at this point you might be feeling a buzz of possibility around entrepreneurship, I encourage you to move slowly through your internal dialogue about what level of entrepreneurial energy is right for you, and in what venue it's best exercised. Taking on a level of entrepreneurship that is too far outside of your current comfort zone can undo the sense of control you have worked hard to build over the course of this book. If you feel unclear, start by harnessing your entrepreneurial energy within the context of your current role and take it from there.

In Chapter One, I talked about how each of the strategies in this book builds on the others to create a way forward for your career, in spite of a challenging job market. You have now explored adopting a gig mindset, identifying your professional value proposition, cultivating your skills, nurturing your social network, and capitalizing on all these career ownership and empowerment strategies by harnessing your entrepreneurial energy.

Let's put all these pieces together now to explore the way forward: the Finch Effect.

# 7

# the finch effect

B y now I am sure you know what I meant at the start of the first chapter when I said that this is not just a career book. At its heart, this is book is about our capacity to adapt as modern professionals and modern humans. If you take one thing away from reading *The Finch Effect,* I want it to be the belief that you have the power to own and direct your career path. It's your birthright.

Yet after speaking with professionals around the country, I have the feeling that somewhere, over the last few years since the recession started, we've forgotten that the ability to evolve ourselves—to be leaders, not followers in our own lives—is found in our very DNA. We are creatures of this earth, and part of the very nature of this earth is change, adaptation, and growth. Darwin wasn't the first to discover this, though he framed it in a new and incredibly useful way.

I'll be honest: over the course of my journey putting this book together, I've often felt irrationally envious of the finches.

While I can't presume to know what is in their little bird brains, I imagine it isn't the complex tangle of frustration, determination, awareness, and accomplishment I and many other professionals often feel as we struggle not just to survive but to thrive in the modern job market. We doubt ourselves and our place in the world of work. Our perceptions shift, get stuck, and often blind us to our full capabilities. I picture the simplicity and matter-of-factness of the finches' perspective as though they were feathery Yodas: "Adapt . . . or do not Adapt. There is no Try."

And yet for all the anxiety, insecurity, and discomfort of change, you have chosen to adapt. You have started asking yourself the right questions about your career. You have developed an adaptive professional brand and started cultivating the skills to match. You have transformed your social media profiles into a promotional venue for your brand, and you are incorporating entrepreneurial strategies into your professional strategies.

## the challenges of ongoing evolution

In many ways, successfully implementing all the strategies within this book and joining the Fittest at the top of the food chain is just the beginning of your work. Once you get to the top, you will need to fight to stay there; not fight against other people—as we learned in the first chapter, survival of the fittest is not about domination and aggressive competition—but instead fight to maintain your perspective, manage your time, continue cultivating your psychological resilience, and practice self-care.

## Perspective

Humans are curious creatures in the sense that our struggle for professional evolution is waged almost entirely internally. If perspective is responsible for 90 percent of how well we adapt, then 90 percent of our fight for vocational survival occurs in the space between our two ears. As you fight to maintain your position as a member of the Fittest, you will need to anticipate and prepare to tackle the mental challenges that will threaten your transformation.

What I've learned on my journey of connecting with extraordinary people around the country is that the quest to thrive is ongoing for even the fittest among us. In spite of our innate ability to change, change (even in its good forms) is hard to work through and even harder to maintain. In Chapter Two, you learned about Renee's transformation from recession casualty to member of the Fittest as she adopted a gig mindset to reclaim ownership of her career. Now that she's made that mental shift, is it all easygoing in the perspective department? "No way," she says. "I have my good days and the days where I have to really work to maintain that perspective. They'll be bad economic news or a tough jobs report and I'll start feeling out of control about my career. The good news is I just need to get some quiet time to do a mini-reframe by asking myself some basic questions to get back on track. But it's definitely a process, not a destination."

One of the biggest challenges for sustaining change is complacency. All members of the Fittest face it. Complacency is the antithesis of adaptation; it is a static, sedentary state of being. When you are complacent, you stop where you are to enjoy your position and relax the push forward. But adaptation is change incarnate, a never ending movement forward that doesn't slow down and doesn't wait. The tradeoff for thriving is a constant vigilance and dedication to your evolution within your changing environment.

After reading this book, you are probably excited to apply the Finch Effect strategies to your career and to see them in action. But will you still be on the path to thriving in six months? Twelve months? Eighteen months? Or will your mindset slip back into that of the unempowered employee, waiting for something to change? Will you consciously promote your brand, or will you again allow other people to classify you with just a few descriptors?

My hope and expectation is that you will maintain the changes in perspective and strategy you have made. You are certainly capable of it. And there will be other, major job market shifts within your lifetime that will call upon members of the Fittest to again lead the way by using the skills we explored in this book: redefining a sense of self as a professional, taking control of your career and brand message, independently developing your skills, sharing your story and differentiation with others, and tapping into your entrepreneurial potential.

And there will also be other, more minor yet more frequent adjustments in the job market that will reward those who can be open to change, aware of their environment, and driven to succeed. In these times of relative calm, it behooves the members of the Fittest to share their knowledge and pass on their strategies to those in their families or professional industries. The teaching and transfer of knowledge not only powerfully maintains your focus on these strategies but also fulfills a basic evolutionary requirement: the passing of successful traits to the next generation.

You are evolving into a leader within your own career and in so doing are providing leadership to those around you. An underlying truth of the Finch Effect is that we do not evolve simply for ourselves; we also evolve for those who are a few steps behind us in their vocational journey. As a member of the Fittest, you are leading the way into the job market of tomorrow and providing a path forward for your colleagues, friends, and perhaps even children.

## Time

Another impediment to maintaining and sharing these strategies is fitting them into our chronically tight schedules. Adopting strategies to manage time is a key component of maintaining success. In Chapter Four, you met Crystal and learned how she used social media to advance her APB and weather an unexpected layoff. For members of the Fittest like her who leverage social media daily, managing time can be the biggest challenge. It is easy to lose track of the distinction between productive and nonproductive when you're measuring in tweets and status updates. Here are two simple yet effective tips for balancing your development as a member of the Fittest with your other responsibilities.

**Make Your Workspace Distraction-Proof.** It doesn't matter if you are working in a home office, workshop, or studio; you need to make sure the space is free from distraction. Resist adding too many things that only serve to divert attention, such as a television or acres of wall art. I can't tell you what will be a distraction for you, as everyone is different; you need to remain aware of what pulls your focus away from your work and keep a list of it. After a month, make an effort to correct these distractions by adjusting your space accordingly or perhaps even moving it. Continue this process each month until you are able to maintain focus without issue.

**End the E-mail Addiction.** E-mail can be a major distraction, especially if you get some kind of a notification that allows you to see when a new message comes into your mailbox. Furthermore, we have all been brainwashed into thinking that hours of e-mailing is work, when really we know it is busy-work. Restrain yourself to checking your e-mail once every hour and a half, at the most. The world won't fall apart if you don't answer each e-mail as soon as it comes in, and you will be pleasantly surprised at how much more productive you can be.

Managing time is essential to managing stress, which can be the number one enemy to those who are working to maintain or advance a change.

## Resilience

Another significant task members of the Fittest face is the continued building of their psychological resilience to bolster their response to the near constant stressors and shocks of life and work. As we discussed in Chapter Four, skill development is not a onetime event. It is a continual quest to keep your skills up to date, relevant, and in use. Skill development is a lot like physical training: you do not just do twenty pushups and walk around for the rest of your life with killer biceps—you need to work on those muscles regularly and introduce new techniques to keep them at the level you want them. Skill development is the same way. And resilience is a life skill.

In addition to the perspective-shifting tactics from Chapter Two, I recommend you continue to use the following APA-approved resilience tactics to improve your ability to cope with stress and maintain the changes you have worked so hard to make. These tactics ask you to call upon work you have already started over the course of the Finch Effect, so you can kill two birds (hopefully not finches) with one stone by building out your resilience and working on your strategies.

**Move Toward Your Goals.** As a member of the Fittest, you have outlined some key goals for yourself in communicating your adaptive professional brand and building out your differentiating and centerpiece skills. To keep yourself on track, consider mapping out a three-month goal schedule that includes time during your week to move toward these objectives. Or break each goal down into its smallest parts and schedule yourself to complete one small part every day. For example, if your goal is to set up your social media profile, set the smaller goal "register for Twitter" as your objective for tomorrow. As the APA notes, "Instead of focusing on tasks that seem unachievable, ask yourself, 'What's one thing I know I can accomplish today that helps me move in the direction I want to go?'"[1]

**Take Decisive Action.** When faced with a difficult career situation, reaffirm your competence and ownership of your career by taking action instead of withdrawing from it. Being a member of the Fittest means moving forward confidently and mindfully into the unknown; waiting on the sidelines for the situation to resolve itself is a trait found in those who are at risk of going extinct.

**Look for Opportunities for Self-Discovery.** The entire journey of the Finch Effect is an opportunity for self-discovery, so I would restate this tactic as "*Continue* to look for opportunities for self-discovery." As we saw on just about every page of this book, adversity is an opportunity for growth and positive

change if we allow ourselves to perceive it that way. (And remember to include those opportunities as part of your
gratitude list!)

## Self-Care

A final, often overlooked challenge for members of the Fittest
is making time for self-care. Self-care refers to the basic
stress-reducing activities we provide ourselves to keep our
batteries charged and our Fittest fires burning. Typically, it
includes things like diet, exercise, sleep, and overall health,
but for some people it can include social time, family time,
or hobby work.

We met Steve in the last chapter; he told us about using his
entrepreneurial energy inside a large financial firm to advance
his APB and cultivate opportunities for himself. Yet his
ongoing success in his new start-up role will depend on his
ability to keep that entrepreneurial fire burning and pushing
him to more innovation and thought leadership. And that
requires self-care. "Finding balance is a big struggle," Steve
notes. "I have to be really careful of not pushing too hard at
work or taking work home every night or every weekend—
something that can be a challenge when I am so interested in
what I'm doing. But I know if I don't make time for some other
things, like sleep, I won't have as much to bring to this work."

While you might not realize it, self-care is a foundational
part of an effective career strategy. Why? Because when you
are burnt out, overtired, or overstressed, it reflects not only in
your ability to perform your daily job responsibilities but also
in your ability to adapt through managing stress.

Ironically, self-care is the first thing that goes when stress
levels increase, because the demands of external elements, like

a job search or role requirements or even the transformative work it takes to become a member of the Fittest, can easily be perceived as more important or urgent. The result is that there is less of us to go around, both for ourselves and for those who depend on us in and out of the workplace.

When you are blazing the trail for the next iteration of the job market, making sure your energy is in top form is a prerequisite for success. I do not expect you to read the following list of self-care tactics and immediately start doing them all—heck, I don't get a chance to do them all every week. But read through them with the intention of implementing one of them—just one—in your upcoming week.

**Don't Skimp on Sleep.** I don't know about you, but the first self-care element that I let go of when I am stressed is sleep. When stressed, I sleep at odd hours, for just a few hours, then wake up and get back to work. The result over a few days of this is a pervasive mental fog, drained energy, and bags under my eyes that make me look like I belong in a zombie movie. I know I am not alone when it comes to sleep sacrifice. All I have to do is look on Google Chat at three in the morning to realize there is a whole army of compromised sleepers out there. That doesn't bode well for our ability to perform.

If you have a history of skimping on sleep, I recommend you take the time to identify a sleep program that makes sense for you and your lifestyle and then schedule it into your calendar accordingly. And I do mean this literally: if your schedule interferes with a regular sleep program, pencil sleep in, and even better, set a reminder alarm to notify you when it's time to pack up whatever you are doing and hit the hay. Try this tactic for a minimum of five days to experience a significant refresh in your energy levels.

**Eat for Energy.** Make sure you are getting adequate amounts of essential nutrients in your diet on a regular basis to keep your energy levels high and your mind clear. Just like with sleep, everyone's body is different, so take some time to experiment with what combinations of fruits, vegetables, whole grains, protein, and dairy work to keep your engine running throughout your day.

**Exercise Your Mind and Body.** Make time for physical exercise and reap the mental rewards as well. Exercising your body helps to relieve stress, improve sleep, and regulate emotions. Additionally, it can provide much needed quiet time in your mind to work on building your resilience and resetting your perspective. If you struggle to find time to exercise regularly, use your sleep technique and put it in your calendar. Once it is there, treat it like you would treat a client appointment, and honor it.

**Rest, Relax, and Recoup.** If you are sick with a cold or run-down or just need a break, be sure you give yourself permission to rest, relax, and recuperate. One of the worst things most of us do when we are overloaded is try to push through fatigue or illness instead of stopping to deal with it. Our physical, mental, and emotional resources are rechargeable, but they are by no means infinite. Stop to refill the gas tank when it's low, or be prepared to sit by the side of the road (which literally manifests as the flu, migraines, or a breakdown) and wait for AAA.

The key to successfully implementing all these self-care tactics is allowing yourself to make it a priority. Here's the truth: if you don't put yourself and the needs of your personal resources first, no one else will. In this challenging economy it is imperative that we show up every day running on all cylinders, not just to keep our heads above water but to be able to spot those special opportunities that are visible only to members of the Fittest.

## understanding the finch effect

In 2009, I set out to find the people in America who were successfully advancing their careers in spite of the challenging job market. My goal was simply to get a few pointers and strategies I could share with my friends and family so we would all get through this rough economic time in one piece. Instead, I ended up with a set of universal strategies and a real sense of awe for our human ability to lead our own personal transformations.

What has surprised me the most is that in an attempt to neutrally report on what it takes to thrive in our modern job market, I have been brought into the world of the Fittest and learned about their strategies right alongside you. I suppose I shouldn't be that surprised, because just like the Galápagos finches, we are all on our own evolutionary paths as similar yet distinctive professionals. We do not need to step on each other, or beat each other down, or climb over one another to earn the title of the Fittest; we simply need to take ownership of our future and draw from our unique set of experiences and skills to stand out and make a place for ourselves. There is something hopeful and promising about the thought that wherever this job market is going there is room to succeed. We just need to be alert and ready to seize our opportunities.

My hope is that in reading this book, you have found as much value in these lessons and strategies as I have. It is hard to find a way to effectively end the work we have done together over the course of *The Finch Effect*, because it isn't an ending at all—it is a beginning. It is the beginning of a new career for you, even if you stay in the same job. So I want to send you out on your journey with one final word of advice: don't look back to your previous, pre-Fittest existence in anger or frustration, because you could never have come to this place without your past experiences. Everything happens for a reason, and you may never know how the struggles and challenges of the past few years prepared you for the next steps in your career. As they say, it is the *journey* that matters in the end. So here's to your journey, wherever it may lead you, and I wish for you nothing less than luck, success, and the ability to channel your inner finch for years to come.

Sometimes I like to think about young Darwin standing on the deck of *HMS Beagle*, half excited and half nervous as the ship moved toward the open sea. As the December wind lashed him, he wasn't worried about what he would discover or the fact that he was untrained in most of the duties he was to perform on the trip. He was off on a long-desired adventure away from his family and their expectations, completely unaware of how the voyage was to affect his life, and the course of the world. He was scanning the horizon for the next unknown, eager to tackle it head-on, and open to the experience.

This is the Finch Effect.

# notes

## Chapter 1

1. Desmond, A., and Moore, J. *Darwin: The Life of a Tormented Evolutionist.* New York: W. W. Norton, 1991.
2. *Ibid.*, 169.
3. *Ibid.*, 172.
4. Urquhart, M. A., and Hewson, M. A. "Unemployment Continued to Rise in 1982 as Recession Deepened," *Monthly Labor Review Online,* 1983, 106(2). http://www.bls.gov/opub/mlr/1983/02/art1exc.htm
5. Hilsenrath, J., and Dougherty, C. "Inside the Disappointing Comeback," *Wall Street Journal,* July 15, 2011. http://online.wsj.com/article/SB10001424052702304760604576425793342142396.html
6. Smith, N. F. "The New Job Market: Who Wins and Who Loses?" CBS MoneyWatch, June 24, 2009. http://moneywatch.bnet.com/retirement-planning/article/the-new-job-market-who-wins-and-who-loses/314930/
7. "CFO Survey: Optimism Tumbles, Employment Picture Bleak," Duke Today. September 15, 2010. http://today.duke.edu/2010/09/

cfo.html; Woolhouse, M. "Part-Time Workers on Rise in Mass." *Boston Globe*, September 26, 2011. http://articles.boston.com/2011-09-26/business/30205000_1_part-time-jobs-andrew-sum-under employed-workers

8. Doyle, A. "Where Have All the Jobs Gone?" *About.com*.http://jobsearch.about.com/cs/careerresources/a/offshore.htm; Daga, V., and Kaka, N. "Taking Offshoring Beyond Labor Cost Savings," *McKinsey Quarterly*, June 19, 2006. http://www.cfo.com/article.cfm/7054575?f=related; Wessel, D. "Big U.S. Firms Shift Hiring Abroad," *Wall Street Journal*, April 19, 2011. http://online.wsj.com/article/SB10001424052748704821704576270783611823972.html?KEYWORDS=jobs+overseas

9. Wang, J. "Ask a Pro: Employees, Who Needs 'Em?" *Entrepreneur*, March 2010, 18.

10. Brown, T. "The Gig Economy," TheDailyBeast.com, January 12, 2009. http://www.thedailybeast.com/blogs-and-stories/2009-01-12/the-gig-economy/full/

11. *Ibid.*

12. Pink, D. *Free Agent Nation: The Future of Working for Yourself.* New York: Hatchette Book Group, 2001, 12.

13. Locke, E., and Lantham, G. P. *A Theory of Goal Setting and Task Performance.* New York: Prentice Hall College Division, 1990.

## Chapter 2

1. Hart, W., Albarracín, D., Eagly, A. H., Brechan, I., Lindberg, M. J., and Merrill, L. "Feeling Validated Versus Being Correct: A Meta-Analysis of Selective Exposure to Information," *Psychological Bulletin*, 2009, 135(4), 555–588.

2. Zweig, J. "How to Ignore the Yes-Man in Your Head," *Wall Street Journal*, November 19, 2009. http://online.wsj.com/article/SB10001424052748703811604574533680037778184.html

3. American Psychological Association. *The Road to Resilience.* http://www.apa.org/helpcenter/road-resilience.aspx

4. *Ibid.*

5. Archer, S. "The Secret to Lowering Blood Pressure with Breathing Exercises," ABC World News, September 6, 2010. http://abcnews .go.com/WN/secret-lowering-blood-pressure-breathing-exercises/ story?id=11656769

6. Emmons, R. A., and McCullough, M. E. "Counting Blessings Versus Burdens: An Experimental Investigation of Gratitude and Subjective Well-Being in Daily Life," *Journal of Personality and Social Psychology*, 2003, (84)2, 377–389; Peterson, C., Stephens, J. P., Park, N., Lee, F., and Seligman, M.E.P. "Strengths of Character and Work," in P. A. Linley, S. Harrington, and N. Garcea (eds.), *Oxford Handbook of Positive Psychology and Work* (221–231). New York: Oxford University Press, 2010.

7. Fredrickson, B. *Positivity: Top-Notch Research Reveals the 3-1 Ratio That Will Change Your Life.* New York: Three Rivers Press, 2009.

8. American Psychological Association. *The Road to Resilience.* http://www.apa.org/helpcenter/road-resilience.aspx

9. "Positive Thinking: Reduce Stress by Eliminating Negative Self-Talk," Mayo Clinic Online. http://www.mayoclinic.com/health/ positive-thinking/SR00009

10. *Ibid.*

11. Wright, J. H. "Cognitive Behavior Therapy: Basic Principles and Recent Advances," *Focus,* 2006, (4), 173–178.

12. The original derivative of the quote "How then shall we live?" is a biblical verse (2 Peter 3:11): "Since everything will be destroyed in this way, what kind of people ought you be?" While I was first exposed to it in a college lecture, the quote and concept has been used many times throughout the ages.

## Chapter 3

1. Tjan, A. K. "Your Employees Have No Clue What Your Company Does," HBR Blog Network, September 3, 2009.

http://blogs.hbr.org/tjan/2009/09/your-employees-have-no-clue-wh.html

2. Darwin, C. *On the Origin of Species*, New York: Signet Classics, 2003, 77.

3. Doyle, A. "Your Professional Brand: How to Create a Professional Brand," About.com Guide: Job Searching. http://jobsearch.about.com/od/careeradviceresources/a/profbrand.htm

4. Susan Walaszek, founder of HR Compliance Consulting, personal interview with Nacie Carson, September 3, 2011.

5. Pink, D. *Free Agent Nation: The Future of Working for Yourself.* New York: Hatchette Book Group, 2001.

6. Susan Walaszek, founder of HR Compliance Consulting, personal interview with Nacie Carson, September 3, 2011.

7. Sinek, S. "How Great Leaders Inspire Action," TED.com, September 2009. http://www.ted.com/talks/simon_sinek_how_great_leaders_inspire_action.html

8. Stossel, J., and Kendall, K. "The Psychology of Stereotypes," ABC, 20/20, September 15, 2006. http://abcnews.go.com/2020/story?id=2442521&page=1

9. Williams, J. R. "Guidelines for the Use of Multimedia in Instruction," *Proceedings of the Human Factors and Ergonomics Society 42nd Annual Meeting*, 1998, 1447–1451.

#### Chapter 4

1. "Transtheoretical Model," ProChange Behaviors, Inc. http://www.prochange.com/ttm

#### Chapter 5

1. U.S. Census Bureau. "U.S. and World Population Clocks." http://www.census.gov/main/www/popclock.html; "Statistics," Facebook. http://www.facebook.com/press/info.php?statistics; McMillian, G. "Twitter Reveals Active User Number: How Many Actually Say Something," Techland.com, September 9, 2011. http://techland

.time.com/2011/09/09/twitter-reveals-active-user-number-how-many-actually-say-something/; Reisinger, D. "LinkedIn Hits 100 Million Users," CNet.com, March 22, 2011. http://news.cnet.com/8301-13506_3-20045851-17.html

2. Willis, P. "Prince: World Exclusive Interview," Mirror.co.uk, May 7, 2010. http://www.mirror.co.uk/celebs/news/2010/07/05/prince-world-exclusive-interview-peter-willis-goes-inside-the-star-s-secret-world-115875-22382552/

3. John Haydon, founder of Inbound Zombie, personal interview with Nacie Carson, September 26, 2011.

4. Van Grove, J. "Library of Congress to Preserve Tweets for Eternity." Mashable.com, April 14, 2010. http://mashable.com/2010/04/14/twitter-library-of-congress/?utm_source=feedburner&utm_medium=feed&utm_campaign=Feed%3A+Mashable+%28Mash able%29&utm_content=Twitter

5. American Psychological Association. *The Road to Resilience*. http://www.apa.org/helpcenter/road-resilience.aspx

6. Machlis, S. "Facebook vs. Twitter vs. LinkedIn vs. Google+," Computerworld.com, July 11, 2011. http://blogs.computerworld.com/18603/facebook_vs_twitter_vs_linkedin_vs_google_plus

7. *Ibid.*

8. Matyszczyk, C. "Facebook Messes Up Your GPA," CNet.com, April 12, 2009. http://news.cnet.com/8301-17852_3-10217704-71.html

## Chapter 6

1. Wadhwa, V. "Five Myths About Entrepreneurs," *Washington Post*, July 29, 2011. http://www.washingtonpost.com/opinions/five-myths-about-entrepreneurs/2011/06/29/gIQALtCBhI_story.html

2. Locke, E. A. "Toward a Theory of Task Motivation and Incentives," *Organizational Behavior and Human Performance*, 1968, 3(2), 157–189.

3. Roberta Chinsky Matuson, president of Human Resource Solutions, interview with Nacie Carson, September 24, 2009.
4. Howard Stephen Berg, "the world's fastest reader," interview with Nacie Carson, October 20, 2009.
5. Petrecca, L. "Fewer People Choose to Be Self-Employed," *USA Today*, September 9, 2011. http://www.usatoday.com/money/smallbusiness/story/2011-09-07/Fewer-people-choose-to-be-self-employed/50305432/1

## Chapter 7

1. American Psychological Association. *The Road to Resilience.* http://www.apa.org/helpcenter/road-resilience.aspx

# acknowledgments

The three-year journey of researching and writing *The Finch Effect* has been a journey of self-discovery, growth, and joy. This journey, with all its wonder and excitement, would not have been possible without the support and guidance of many amazing and talented people who believed in the message and believed in me.

First, I would like to thank my editor, Genoveva Llosa, and the wonderful team at Jossey-Bass. Thank you, Genoveva, for helping me turn my vision for this book into a reality—your insights and perspective made all the difference. Thank you as well to John Maas for your support and input; working with you was a real pleasure!

I am forever grateful to my literary agent, Linda Konner, who believed in what I had to say and found a home for my idea. Linda, you worked patiently with me as I developed this book and made one of my major life dreams come true; I thank you from the bottom of my heart.

This book would not exist today if it weren't for my incredible support network of family and friends. I will never be able to sufficiently thank my parents, David and Shelley Carson, for all they did to make opportunities like this possible for me. I am blessed to have amazing parents who taught me the value of hard work, determination, and pursuing a career you love. Daddy, thank you for teaching me integrity, discipline, and achievement, and Meem, thank you for teaching me grace, strength, and creativity.

A special thanks is in order for Charles, the love of my life, who helped me maintain faith in myself and my message throughout this process, including my good days and my not-so-good days. *Amor*, you have brought so much light and love into my life I never thought possible. Thank you for your gentle, strong heart.

Thank you to my brother Dave and my two *amigas*, Annie and Renee, for helping me keep joy and laughter in this process. I am blessed to have family members that I think of as best friends, and best friends whom I think of as family.

I'd also like to acknowledge and thank two individuals who have been instrumental in my growth as both a professional and a person. First, thanks to Frank DuMar, CEO of Cleaver Company, for his mentorship and support over the last few years. You have helped me develop as a leader, and I am grateful for the opportunities you have given me. Second, a sincere thanks to Ross Beales Jr., my college advisor, who guided me from Day One through my decisions as a history major, thesis writer, and youngster trying to find her way in the world. Guy, you not only helped bring my writing and critical thinking to the next level but also taught me to trust my instincts and perception of the world. All of those skills have stayed with me long after graduation, and they will remain.

Thank you to everyone whom I spoke with, interviewed, and bounced ideas off for this book. From the Fittest who shared their stories, to the industry experts who patiently shared their insights, to the good friends and online peers who listened to me and gave feedback on the material—I am grateful for your time, energy, and insights!

This book couldn't end without acknowledging Charles Darwin for the inspiration his work and his life have provided me. His copious notes and journal entries helped me piece together not only the thoughts of a world-famous scientist but also those of a true individual. Thank you for having the good sense to save your writings for posterity—I hope our digital generation can learn something from this foresight of documentation.

And last but not least, thank you to the finches of the Galápagos. May you continue to grow, thrive, and of course, adapt.

# about the author

Nacie Carson is a professional development author who focuses on career evolution, entrepreneurship, and authenticity. Her eclectic background—which includes historical research, a stint in corporate America, and experience as a young entrepreneur—coupled with her work in leadership development and executive coaching, has given her a unique perspective on how to craft a career and lifestyle that is meaningful, successful, and authentic.

Her writings on career development, life balance, and the gig economy are published regularly at Entrepreneurs-Journey .com and Portfolio.com, as well as at her own site, TheLifeUn common.net. Nacie also serves as the director of development services for Cleaver Company, a boutique professional development firm in the Boston area.

Nacie received her BA in History from the College of the Holy Cross, where she graduated magna cum laude. She is a member of Phi Beta Kappa and Red Sox Nation. She currently lives on Boston's South Shore with the love of her life.

# index